UNBEATABLE LATINAS

VALERIA ALOE

UNBEATABLE LATINAS

A REBELLIOUS APPROACH TO ACHIEVING PROFESSIONAL SUCCESS

Planeta

Original title: *Latinas imparables*

© 2024, Valeria Aloe

Translated by: © Valeria Aloe, with the support of Fernando Avilés García
Interior design: © Juan Carlos González Juárez
Cover credits: © Genoveva Saavedra / aciditadiseño
Cover illustration: © iStock / Hammad Khan y Evgenii Brotsmann
Photograph by the author: © Mike Peters, 2024

All Rights Reserved

© 2024, Editorial Planeta Mexicana, S.A. de C.V.
Bajo el sello editorial PLANETA M.R.
Avenida Presidente Masarik núm. 111,
Piso 2, Polanco V Sección, Miguel Hidalgo
C.P. 11560, Ciudad de México
www.planetadelibros.us

First edition printed: October 2024
ISBN: 978-607-39-1050-7

Total or partial reproduction of this book or its incorporation into a computer system or transmitted in any form or by any means is not permitted, whether electronic, mechanical, photocopying, recording or otherwise, without the prior permission writing from the copyright holders.

The violation of these rights may constitute an offense against intellectual property. (Arts. 229 and following of the Ley Federal del Derecho de Autor and Arts. 424 and following of the Código Penal Federal)

If you need a photocopy or scanning of some part of this work, please address at CeMPro. (Centro Mexicano de Protección y Fomento de los Derechos de Autor, http://www.cempro.org.mx).

Printed in the workshops of Bertelsmann Printing Group USA.
25 Jack Enders Boulevard, Berryville, Virginia 22611, USA.
Printed in U.S.A.

*To our ancestors,
whose sacrifices paved the way
for us to be where we are today.
In their honor,
may we grant ourselves permission
to fully enjoy our own journey.*

Index

Introduction 13

PART I. We Are Not Victims

1. Powerful, yet powerless 25
2. Rebel against cultural scripts 35
3. Latina sisters, are we united? 51
4. Colorism: How we deny our history 62
5. Relegated and fighting for crumbs 74

PART II. Understand the Rules

6. Change starts within you 89
7. Can you succeed by being yourself? 104
8. Break the silence and talk about yourself . 123
9. Dare to go for more 139

PART III. Master Your Game

10. From one to many, a turning point 159
11. Your career or your family? 175

12. Your future is not only in your hands 194
13. Sponsors: Our missing link 211

PART IV. Rewrite the Rules

14. Be part of the change. 229
15. Push up and pull up. 242
16. Our unity, a utopia? 258
17. Create the third culture 269

Conclusion 284
Acknowledgments. 288
Bibliography 291
About the author 301

Due to the complexity of repetitively using each of the terms Latinas, Latinos, Hispanics, Latinx, and Latine throughout this book, the author has simplified their use under the terms Latinas and Latinos. In this way, she respectfully seeks to represent the diverse groups that make up our community while maintaining literary fluidity.

Introduction

It's three in the morning on a freezing cold night in February of 2016 in New Jersey. I find myself in the darkest hour of the night, as dark as this moment I am going through. As the daughter of a working-class family and the first to access college education and corporate jobs in top-tier companies, I did everything to succeed in spaces foreign to my humble beginnings. I pushed so hard, sacrificing myself beyond what was humanly possible, that I ended up falling into an unprecedented physical, mental, and emotional burnout.

For decades, I had bowed my head to internal and external voices of disapproval while carrying my immigrant accent as a secret source of shame, feeling at every step that I should be grateful for being allowed to live in this country even though I was here legally. In my effort to shut down the inner uncomfortable turbulence that I experienced living within a system that never quite accepted me, I took refuge in what I knew to do best, what I had learned from our Latino culture: work hard.

The consequences were disastrous, and my dark and deep fall into a void was almost inevitable. I reached a turning point in my life and things would no longer be the same. I was broken inside. In the silence of that night, I contained a cry of helplessness to avoid waking my family up, and tears flowed down my cheeks. I wondered when this nightmare would end. I no longer knew who I was or where I was going.

After 15 years in the United States, giving it all to feel appreciated, valued, and welcomed, I lost my way. I am sunk in a very different experience from what I imagined when, with big dreams and just a few suitcases, I arrived in this country in 2002 to pursue a master's degree in Business at an Ivy League university. A system and a culture brutally different from where I come from took it upon itself to «put me in my place,» one that feels too small compared to what I imagined myself achieving when I first set foot in this country. I feel inferior, different, and out of place. In this darkness with no end in sight, images from recent past experiences spin furiously around me, and voices coming from deep within drill into my ears with no mercy.

You don't belong here. Deep down, you know you are not one of us. Go back to the country you came from.

No one cares about what you can contribute. Don't forget that you come from a third-world country.

People like you don't get very far, you know? Look around... Do you find Latina women like you in those spaces you have aspired to reach?

I'm sick and tired of these voices and of not feeling at home, welcome, or valued for who I really am after 15 years in this country. I have wasted too much energy trying to be someone different, hoping to receive that external stamp of approval. I have repeatedly placed others and their agendas above my dreams and needs, putting them on pedestals.

A feeling of desperate helplessness joins my profound exhaustion. I push down everything I feel, hiding it somewhere deep inside of me so that no one notices the weight I carry. In the end, «we don't talk about it.» Our culture has taught us to remain silent.

As much as I try, I cannot make myself fit into a model of success designed for people different than me. The «You will be the first in our family to go to college» and «You will be a source of pride for all of us; you will achieve the dreams of your grandparents» are no longer enough for me to keep pushing forward. I am at a turning point in my life. Suddenly, a very faint voice whispers within me that perhaps, one day, things could be different.

* * *

—Valeria, have you finished covering your topics and projects? —The company's chief operating officer, who I worked with as marketing director, asked me. That was the last corporate job I had before my collapse. I was one of the few women in the company and the only Latina.

—Yes, that's all I had for today. Thank you for your time —I thanked the team of 12 people on the other end of the phone. Conducting that meeting from my home was unusual, but I had no other choice, as my youngest son, then four years old, had developed a sudden overnight fever.

—Very well —said the chief operating officer sharply. He was not only respected by most of the people at the table but also feared—. Now, you can go back to cooking and babysitting.

My silence struck me. I was petrified... Had I heard correctly? Yes, I had. I was left speechless between shame and being caught off guard.

When I recovered a little, that familiar voice inside me said, «Let it go. It's not in your best interest to say anything, or you'll be labeled difficult, hindering your career. In the end, he has much more power than you.»

With that knot in my stomach that showed up every time I swallowed my words and emotions instead of expressing them, I took a deep breath and hung up the call. Months later, I hit rock bottom.

Around the same time, Natalia, who grew up in the United States under the care of her single mother, who had immigrated from Colombia, went through a similar experience.

Natalia was also the first in her family to graduate from college in the United States. She became one of the few Latina engineers in the endless ocean of white men who worked with her at a renowned oil company. Like many of us who are the first in our family to venture into new territories, Natalia did not have a roadmap to guide her steps. But Natalia knew something, and she knew it very well: to succeed, you have to do your job with commitment and attention to detail. You must build trust with your bosses and show them they can assign you projects supporting your growth. Her commitment to exceeding objectives caught the attention of those bosses, who selected her to travel to Munich, Germany, as part of a committee of seven people involved in acquiring state-of-the-art machinery. The trip included six engineers and Natalia, the only woman and Latina in the group.

—What you say is irrelevant; we don't have time for that now. Shut up! I need to think! —the project leader, a Peruvian-American engineer, snapped dismissively. He had interrupted Natalia, who was explaining her thoughts on the possible disadvantages of the equipment they were evaluating.

She felt the sky falling on her. She was as petrified as I had been with that chief operating officer. She had worked very hard to reach that position, encountering resistance at every step from men who were not used to receiving orders and instructions from younger Latina women.

Not knowing what to do, Natalia opted to stay silent, even when she knew this incident would make things even more difficult for her. Her credibility was at stake.

Natalia and I are not alone. And neither are you. At this point, millions of Latina women face these types of situations, in which we tend to take refuge in our cultural behavior of «Put your head down and work harder» and the thought of «Show them what you're capable of with more work and better results.» But this is not sustainable. Our cultural inclination to dedicate more hours and more mental space to work, combined with the exhausting effect of stress and microaggressions, can hurt our mental health.

In the 21st century, Latina women continue operating in survival mode. We survive instead of fully living. With our tendency to work hard and even harder, we force ourselves to keep pushing through when that clearly does not work for us, without knowing exactly what we could be doing differently. With this, we place our mental and physical health at risk, as happened to me in 2016, when, after decades of pressuring myself to succeed in a system where I did not feel welcome, valued, or supported, I collapsed from chronic stress.

If you can relate to my experience or Natalia's, I want you to know that you are not alone. Operating in survival mode is collective and inherited. It is collective since it doesn't matter what our country of origin, skin color, sexual orientation, preferred language, or educational level is. As Latinas, we share that sense of living in survival mode. We carry it as a collective cultural trait that influences our thinking, feeling, and acting. Our survival mode is also inherited because we have been close witnesses of how our ancestors, with few resources, faced significant challenges and traumas, whether in their countries of origin or as immigrants in the United States. Many of them were silenced, minimized, ignored, and even discarded by an American system that did not welcome them with open arms. Their daughters, as may be your case, not only witnessed the dismissive messages towards their parents, but they also had to translate them word for word on numerous occasions. Observing our ancestors' struggles, some believed survival was also our destiny. And because of this, we may carry the unhealed traumas and fears of our ancestors in our DNA, many times unconsciously.

In the encounter of two cultures, one perceived as clearly superior to the other, we absorbed like sponges several messages of inferiority that surfaced when we were compared to the white male model of perfection and success this country historically held. In that exercise of comparison, we wonder if we possess the qualities needed to succeed in this country, we feel uncomfortable when talking about our talents and successes because they seem insufficient, or we take refuge in silence when we face situations that we perceive as threatening, even when doing so can result in being labeled as «not leadership material» or poorly prepared to take our next professional leap. Survival silently follows us into every room and tries to keep us trapped in a past that our mind and heart have not yet unlearned, a past that should no longer determine our destiny.

On that ice-cold night in 2016, I desperately clung to the one thing that could get me out of that hole: my spirituality. For years, I neglected my relationship with that deeper part of my essence, focused on my thirst to prove my worth, and constantly pressured to pursue more. I think this is how I lost my way: I stopped loving myself, valuing myself, and feeling worthy. I put aside my spiritual life to pursue an unattainable perfection and to gain the approval of others when I wasn't even approving of myself.

That night, I changed the course of my life because, in that darkness, I learned to ask for help.

«I would like to know what my next steps are. I need a sign,» I desperately pleaded to the infinite energy I call God, and others call by hundreds of different names. I wondered if anything would work because nothing I had tried so far seemed to make a difference. Where was my way out of all this darkness and of feeling like a failure?

The following morning, when I turned my phone on to check the time, I found two emails that had arrived during the night. The subject line of the first one read «Tell your story,» and the second one said, «Publish a book and leave a legacy.»

And here we are.

The years that followed were not easy. During those years, I looked without filters into everything that led me to collapse.

I embarked on a mission to understand what ways of thinking and behaviors had pushed me to such profound suffering. I immersed myself in decoding the cultural differences that make us feel inadequate and undervalued as immigrants and daughters of immigrants. In the process, I learned to accept that this is indeed my home, my country. I embraced the idea that I belong here and deserve to reach my highest potential and live a happy life. By shedding the layers of cultural conditioning and indoctrination of inferiority, silence, and service to others above all else with which I had grown up, I could reconnect with my true essence, learning to love the person I am and gradually healing my self-esteem and self-worth.

In the process, I was blessed to cross paths with hundreds of Latina women who taught me the most profound life lessons, the ones we generally do not share, either because we are too busy fighting to make our way or because of our scarcity mindset that has us holding on to information that could help others. Hence my decision to leave this legacy for you, mainly if you are the first in your family to navigate spaces that were not accessible to your ancestors or if you find yourself struggling to be accepted, heard, or valued for who you are, like Natalia, like me, and like so many women you will meet throughout pages.

In the following pages, we will embark on the most profound transformative journey together. We will begin by examining our individual and collective shadows, the intergenerational trauma we still carry, and the many ways in which our cultural past continues to influence our present, having us experience unnecessary struggle and suffering. We will then embark on understanding how we can change our reality starting from within, reprogramming our minds to pursue higher-level goals and fulfill our most cherished dreams. I will lay out a detailed roadmap for you, with the specific pillars you need to focus on to take your professional life to levels yet to be reached. And finally, we will wrap up with an exploration of what the future of this country and the world will look like as we, Latinas and

Latinos, dare to bring our most cherished cultural values of authenticity, empathy, caring, loyalty, resilience, joy, and a collective way of thinking into our professional spaces. I will show you how we will be leaders of an unprecedented cultural change.

This book is also for you if you are not Latina or Latino but an ally. You will become aware of our deepest secrets and the silent struggles we do not generally talk about, and you will walk away with insights and a toolkit to support our growth. You are a vital player in helping us reach our maximum potential. Through these pages, you will better understand how to become an agent of change who actively creates a new and powerful collective reality that includes you.

But before we begin our journey together, I want us to dispel the notion that «being Latina is a handicap.» On the contrary, being Latina or Latino is a potent asset. The power of our Latino community is the best-kept secret, with 77% of us not being aware of the immense power we possess.

The irony is that we are mighty but without power. On the one hand, we are a growing segment of the United States population, driving such significant economic contributions that we have become one of the main engines of the American economy. We are resourceful, loyal, resilient, empathetic, entrepreneurial, and leaders. Many of us speak more than one language and simultaneously navigate multiple cultures. However, we are relatively absent in spaces of leadership, decision-making, and wealth creation.

This turns us into a paradox, the Hispanic paradox: we possess measurable and growing power, but we continue to feel like second-class citizens. We go through life almost apologizing before giving our opinion, feeling guilty for asking to be paid market value for our work, or hiding our greatness as we feel constantly threatened.

After my 2016 episode, I bounced back by asking myself a simple but powerful question that today can be the cornerstone of your transformation and growth: Am I a powerless victim of an unfair system that still does not recognize my value? Or is it possible that, in some way, I am a victim of my conditioning, having believed to the letter all those cultural messages of inferiority, silence, service to others above all else, and scarcity?

I hope that the main ideas in this book will profoundly change your thoughts about yourself and the world around you. If you read it with consciousness and take action based on what you learn in each chapter, I promise that at the end of our journey together you will not only feel more seen, heard, and valued, but you will also have connected with a part of yourself that may have gone dormant: your human dignity, which has the power to transform your life and also the system from which you feel alienated or by which you feel threatened. You will present yourself with more confidence, develop your unique voice, and surround yourself with people who want to support your growth as mentors and sponsors. Better yet, you'll have more clarity about what steps to take to help you reach your highest professional potential. Let's not wait any longer.

The world is hungry for leaders and change agents like you and me, willing to transform ourselves first to trigger unprecedented collective change. Here we go!

PART I

We Are Not Victims

CHAPTER 1

Powerful, yet powerless

I loved numbers all my life. In a world with so many shades of gray and nuances, numbers have comforted me, as they generally tell a straightforward story. That's why, after years of exhaustion from living an extreme corporate lifestyle and the uncertainty that followed when I left that space, I turned for comfort to what I knew well: analyzing numbers. I wanted to understand who we are as Latinos, perhaps to understand myself more.

What I discovered was fascinating and paradoxical at the same time. I had lived in the United States for 15 years, navigating elite spaces and top-tier corporations where the economic and social power of the Latino community had never received serious attention. That was so revealing that, from then on, I promised to share those numbers at every opportunity.

And each time, I encountered the same response: an overwhelming silence followed by surprise, indignation, and frustration. It happens at every conference I give, almost without exception. At first, the audience is left speechless, absorbing the robust statistics I present to them, which, on the one hand, confirm the immense power of our Latino community in the United States and, on the other hand, make it clear how little we exercise that power. It is as if our past and present contributions and undoubted influence on the destiny of the United States did not exist or did not matter. I learned that our facts and figures are simply unknown to the majority of the 340 million inhabitants of this country, including ourselves. We are powerful, yet powerless.

IGNITE YOUR POWER

Latinas are a fast-growing group in the United States. Approximately 25 years ago, we represented 13% of the female population in this country. Today, we represent 19%, or approximately 30 million. If you consider the more than twenty countries that makeup Latin America, only two of them exceed this number of women among their inhabitants: Brazil and Mexico. In the United States, we are one of the groups with the highest population growth; by 2050, Latinas will represent 26% of the female population; that is, one in four women you cross on the street will be Latina.

How different life could be for my U.S.-born children by the time they become adults! Nowadays, when my family feels the need to be embraced by our cultural warmth, we travel to Miami for a few days. We enjoy our food, listen to our music, and immerse ourselves in a world that speaks our language. It is quite a different experience from the one we live in the suburbs of New Jersey, in a town that is more than 90% non-Latino white. Numbers show that in the near future, we might not have to travel so far to find that connection with our own culture. We will be everywhere.

Moreover, our youth is coming in full force. Did you know that a Latina woman in the United States turns 18 every sixty seconds? Because of that, we are entering the workforce faster than other groups. And while Latinas represent 8% of the U.S. workforce today, our participation in it will grow by 26% by 2030, nearly nine times the projected growth for non-Latina white women. Hence, it is essential to support our youth and make their journey a little easier than it has been for us.

Numbers tell a fascinating story that does not end here. The economic contributions of the Latino community are significant and valuable: we are the undoubted engine of the American economy. The term that quantifies it, the Latino GDP (GDP for Gross Domestic Product), represents the added value to the economy from all goods and services produced by Latinas and Latinos in the United States. In 2021, the Latino GDP amounted to $3.2 trillion. Seen from another perspective, if Latinos in the United States agreed to form our own country, with this gross domestic product, we would be... (please, take a seat before continuing to read)... the fifth largest economy in the world and the third fastest growing, according to a report by the Latino Donor Collaborative. Do you understand why it is incomprehensible that we ask for permission to express ourselves and own our spaces? In the United States, no other ethnic or racial group contributes to the same accelerated growth we create. This country needs us Latinas and Latinos to continue being the world's leading economy that it is.

Latina women are creating businesses at a higher pace than non-Latina white women. In other words, we are a perfect example of what pursuing our big dreams means, and we are role models in perseverance and resilience. According to a report by American Express, in the last five years, the number of businesses created by Latina women grew by 40%, compared to only 6% for non-Latina white women. Latinas know that owning our own business can be a way out of poverty and an opportunity to get ahead.

It all sounds lovely up to this point. Let's now consider the other side of the coin.

THE HISPANIC PARADOX

Given these powerful statistics, the fact that we are absent from spaces of power, decision-making, and wealth creation is astonishing and unacceptable. Finding Latina women in leadership positions is very uncommon. In fact, we occupy less than 2% of executive positions in the largest companies in the country, and we are underrepresented in managerial positions (accounting for only 4%) and professional roles (we reach only 3%). Of the 92 S&P 100 companies analyzed in a recent report, 18 do not have one Latina woman in these positions.

Not only are we relatively absent from leadership positions, but we also make less money than our peers. Throughout my corporate career, I always suspected that some of my colleagues, who had less global experience and fewer academic degrees than me, earned more for a similar job. In 2004 —my first year working in this country— I learned how men around me received a higher salary or annual bonus than mine. Of course, I swallowed my frustration and disappointment and said nothing about it. After all, I was a newcomer and had to pay my dues without complaining. At least, that is what I believed at the time. Regarding salaries and wealth creation, Latina women are far behind other groups. In 2022, full-time Latina professionals were paid approximately 54 cents for every dollar a non-Latino white man earned. Half! This wage gap translates into a loss of nearly 1.2 million dollars that we fail to earn over a forty-year career. In other words, a Latina woman would have to work until she is almost 90 years old, which is six years beyond her life expectancy, to be paid the same total amount of money that a 60-year-old non-Latino white man earned throughout his life.

Latina women are saving less and accumulating insufficient wealth, leaving a smaller inheritance and sometimes a negative balance and accumulated bills to be paid by our families. In that sense, our upcoming generations are at a disadvantage: statistics indicate that a Latino household has only 21 cents of accumulated wealth for every dollar of wealth in the hands of non-Latino white households.

Something very similar happens with Latina entrepreneurs. Our businesses reach annual revenues that account for only

23% of what a similar business owned by a non-Latina white woman generates. We are opening new businesses at fast rates but growing a little in sales.

In summary, we are very powerful, much more than we believe, but we do not fully exercise that power, nor are we accumulating enough wealth to feel deserving of that power. Worse yet, we can fear exercising our power, expecting negative consequences.

Welcome to the Hispanic paradox.

100% RESPONSIBILITY

This is where I place my finger on the wound to invite us to reflect on how we are 100% responsible for the reality we are immersed in. We are not mere victims of an unjust system, but rather, we end up creating a reality that does not favor us each time we walk into our daily lives trapped in a smaller version of ourselves, filled with doubts, feeling undervalued, and influenced by our cultural scripts of silence, invisibility, inferiority, and service to others above all else.

I promised you that I would transform your way of thinking. Here we go with one of the main concepts: we have 100% responsibility for what goes on in our lives, and this can be quite different from what we were culturally taught. When you are 100% responsible, you are not a helpless victim of life's circumstances; instead, you accept that you create, promote, or allow what happens in your life.

A part of you screams, «But the system is unfair!» and «Discrimination is real!» You are absolutely right. The system has not shown significant changes in access and representation of Latinas and Latinos since the 1980s, and bias is real and perverse.

It took me a long time to fully understand this concept. Think about the chief operating officer who humiliated me in front of my co-workers or Natalia when she was silenced in front of other engineers. Neither she nor I were victims of those circumstances. Somehow, we created, allowed, or promoted them. In my desperate attempt to be accepted by others, I allowed jokes that seemed innocent until they escalated, and when I wanted to set boundaries, it was too late. My bosses and my colleagues took advantage of my kindness, as they knew I would not react negatively and there would be no consequences for them, and they took those spaces I left open to channel their masked racism and machismo.

Like many other women, we were taught to promote peaceful relationships, be pleasant, not go against the tide, and serve others before ourselves. That's why setting boundaries in situations that don't favor us can feel uncomfortable and unnatural. I know I allowed it over and over again. Many times, even with a smile on my face!

It would be easier to assign the blame for our lack of access and opportunities to the current government, the system, the non-Latino white community, men with not much consciousness and awareness, or our bosses or co-workers. But what do we gain from doing so? We will feel helpless and angry, but that state changes absolutely nothing.

ACT OF HEALTHY REBELLION

Take paper and pencil and write:

«Today, (add day, month, and year), I, (add your full name), decide to take the helm of my life and choose to be 100% responsible for my actions and results.»

Place this paper in a visible place to remind yourself during challenging days of the commitment you just made and to see your life from a completely different angle, one of 100% responsibility.

Think about the microaggressions that have marked your professional life. How many have you allowed and why? Maybe you wanted to protect your work relationships and feared being fired or losing a client. All of that is valid. It is also valid to realize that, by not setting boundaries, we have been, to some extent, responsible for the permanence of those events in our lives. Responsibility is not about blaming or punishing ourselves but recognizing our ability to respond. Instead of standing idly in the face of challenging events, we accept that we are influential creators of our reality by responding to situations we do not like. So, according to this concept, the fact that your current circumstances are not exactly as you would like them to be or that you are immersed in a system that seems not to accept you as you are or welcome your points of view and contributions does not mean that you cannot do anything about it.

There is an exception to the 100% responsibility rule. There are circumstances in which we are victims of trauma or violence, where we have no control over the actions of other people, particularly during our early years of life. In these cases, you are responsible for only one thing: seeking help to heal and to live fully, just as you deserve. If you have been a victim of trauma or violence, allow yourself to access professional help or other resources so that you can heal.

EXERCISE YOUR (HEALTHY) REBELLIOUSNESS

Accepting that you have the power to create positive events and circumstances in your life and that you can become an agent of change in this unjust system is an attitude of profound and healthy rebellion against the messages of inferiority, silence, service to others above all else, and scarcity that we have been bombarded with since we have been born.

We Latinas need to rebel a bit more. Not in the sense of going into fight mode and confrontation to hurt others, but in questioning our thinking patterns and what we believed to be accurate. What if we started by rebelling against everything we carry in our subconscious, questioning those ancestral messages that say we are not good enough, that going for more is greedy, or that it is dangerous to be our authentic selves? The psychologist Carl Jung studied this topic in-depth and called it the collective unconscious. According to Jung, group members can share archetypes and mental patterns, which can influence their thoughts, actions, and decisions in pretty similar ways. These mental scripts are passed down from generation to generation without realizing it and can become a potent interference between us and our big dreams.

Some time ago, Verónica, a Latina executive at a well-known global financial services institution, confessed that after reading my first book, *Uncolonized Latinas: Transforming Our Mindsets and Rising Together*, she had finally understood why it had been so tricky for Latina women to reach certain executive positions in the United States. When she became aware of the hidden cultural scripts that influenced her thoughts and decisions and decided to overcome those limiting beliefs, she experienced a remarkable improvement in her professional performance. It finally sank on her that what she had perceived as a personal issue or area to fix about herself was a cultural trait so many of us share. When you change your mindset, your life changes. If you are a mother, father, or teacher and decide to end those mentalities, you will not only transform your life, but you will also break ancestral chains and create an important legacy for future generations.

With our healthy rebellion, awareness, and self-empowerment, we will be modeling to our family, friends, and coworkers (and the 440 million people who will inhabit U.S. soil in 2050) what can be possible for us in human development. Given the growing incidence of the Latino population in the United States, it is worth asking: *What kind of Latinas and Latinos do we want in the United States?* What version of ourselves can benefit this country the most? Disempowered individuals who feel inferior, without access to key spaces, lacking confidence in themselves, and who mistrust the system, or individuals with high self-esteem and self-confidence, who think they belong here and who are willing to fight against systemic barriers to contribute the best of themselves for the highest good of all?

Let's delve together into this historic opportunity to create a new collective future, not only for Latina women and our community but also for all the United States and even other countries worldwide that are looking at our progression as a reference for themselves. The empowerment and awakening of our Latino community is indeed a matter of global interest.

The world needs leaders and change agents like you and me who are 100% responsible for their lives and willing to transform their mindsets and behaviors to promote an unprecedented collective change.

LESSONS LEARNED

- Latina women are an increasingly important segment of the United States. By 2050, we will represent almost 30% of the population.

- Our contributions to the American economy (Latino GDP) are significant, and we create new businesses at disproportionately higher rates.

- Despite our importance and contributions to the economy, we are relatively absent from leadership and wealth creation spaces. This is the Hispanic paradox.

- The concept of 100% responsibility invites us to take the reins of our growth, recognizing that by being powerful creators of what happens in our lives, we also have the power to transform our reality.

- A first step towards change is to become aware that specific messages in our collective unconscious lead us to doubt ourselves, to settle for less, or to believe that it is risky to show our authentic selves.

- A first act of healthy rebellion is questioning thought patterns that delay or impede our growth and perpetuate systemic gaps.

CHAPTER 2

Rebel against cultural scripts

We have been brainwashed for centuries. Generation after generation, like sponges, we absorbed a system of beliefs and cultural scripts that have done nothing but wear us down emotionally, physically, and mentally, in addition to disconnecting us from who we truly are.

The time has come to rebel against everything we were programmed to believe, starting by understanding how specific cultural messages created ways of thinking that have taken root in our collective unconscious and, from there, influence our actions and decisions without us being fully aware. As you progress through the following pages, note what resonates with you. Therein lies the key to creating the change you long for, observing, and becoming aware of what has been limiting you without holding judgments against yourself. And if judgments, guilt, or shame appear, I invite you to breathe deeply and let them go as you exhale. It is impossible to learn and grow if we flog ourselves during the process. Expansion and contraction cannot exist together at the same time.

You will discover that many of these scripts can apply to most women, not just Latinas. However, they do not impact different female groups in the same way. Each culture has its ancestral history and a unique relationship with authority, money, the concept of success, poverty, the acceptance of physical punishment, and gender roles, for example. This means that the impact of these scripts varies from community to community, which has to do with specific cultural beliefs that have influenced us since we were young and the conditions in which we grew up.

THE CULTURAL SCRIPT OF INFERIORITY

Inferiority translates as a feeling of inadequacy or lack. This trait has accompanied me throughout my life.

Feeling less than others (particularly when comparing ourselves to non-Latino white men and women) can be so rooted in our psyche that we can feel it even if our accomplishments have been extraordinary. For example, did you know that just 1% of all women with doctorates (PhDs) in the United States are Latinas? That percentage is meager because we are almost 20% of the population. If you are a Latina and have a doctorate, you are within a group with access to one of the highest levels of education. With that, you are extraordinary in our community. Even then, I have found women within this group who feel inadequate or not so capable. Not even reaching the highest educational levels removes the feeling of not being enough. How often, being highly qualified, do we continue striving for one more degree or certification? When this comes from a place of lack, we don't do it to expand our already excellent profile but to appease that inner feeling that we are not yet enough.

As I mentioned above, this feeling of inferiority is not just unique to Latinas. Some time ago, I connected via phone with a Latina executive who has reached the highest ranks within her organization and now reports directly to the president. She told me about a two-day corporate retreat in which she had participated along with other female executives. While at the beginning of the retreat, they all maintained a politically correct stance in their interventions. During the second day and in a group activity, they were brutally honest: most admitted not feeling prepared to succeed in their role or doubting their abilities to do excellent work. We tend to carry the myth that once we reach leadership positions, we will have more confidence because we will have more power. In reality, unless we heal our feelings of inadequacy, those higher positions will only exacerbate the feeling once we get there. In the case of Latina women, there are also certain intersectionalities, such as skin color or accent, that amplify our sense of being inadequate or less capable than others.

When a system is designed around the success of a specific type of individual, those who do not fit that profile can feel out of place as we climb the ranks. Under these circumstances, women have learned to hide our insecurities, silence our deepest needs, and move forward focused only on business, as so many men do, covering up anything that could make us seem weak or insecure.

In the case of our Latino community, many immigrant women and daughters of immigrants silently carry that feeling of inferiority. Those of us who are immigrants may experience a sense of shame because we come from countries that have been labeled as third-world economies. Coming from systemic poverty can also become a weight on our chests as we navigate new spaces in this first-world country. When I began my master's studies (MBA) in 2002, during my first day at the Tuck School of Business at Dartmouth, the first thing I thought was, «What am I going to contribute here if I come from a third-world country that is broke, has systemic poverty, and has just gone through its most profound economic crisis?» At that time, I thought the United States was a perfect system where everything was figured out, so I had everything to learn and little to contribute. And since I felt inferior, I made myself as invisible as possible.

We may also carry a sense of shame towards our accents when we speak English, without knowing that after the age of

11 or 12, the part of the brain that controls language has, for the most part, already developed; thus, if we learn a second language after that age, it will be challenging to completely erase our accent when speaking it. Our accent shame is heightened when those around us point out that we are somewhat different or insinuate that our way of speaking is a barrier to being understood. When others throw our insecurities in our faces, we feel hurt. The same Latina executive who shared her experience in that eye-opening retreat also told me that in a meeting with a dozen executives, where she was the only Latina, one of her peers alluded to her accent and asked her to speak more slowly and clearly as he did not understand what she wanted to say. She felt humiliated.

For Latina women and other women of color born to immigrants, the feeling of inferiority or inadequacy may also come from what they observed from their parents during childhood. Mónica Martínez Milán, an entrepreneur born in New Jersey to Spanish parents, expresses it very clearly:

> My parents had access to education and understood their value before arriving in the United States, but once here, the system forced them to start from scratch, as if everything they had achieved did not matter. When you observe your immigrant parents feeling diminished in front of American people, even when they had a college education, something happens inside your heart as their daughter. By placing others on pedestals, they automatically put themselves on a lower step. As daughters, we experienced that from our birth. I ended up believing that I was inferior to others. I thought something was wrong with me and that I was less capable or valuable than others.

Inferiority is not just a feeling we carry in silence; it manifests in particular and often unconscious behaviors that can block our professional growth.

Indicate the behaviors with which you most identify:

- I let better opportunities pass me by, feeling that I am not ready for them or will not be able to handle them.
- I only apply for jobs if I meet 100% of the requirements, while statistics show that men apply even when they only meet 60% of the requirements.
- I work too hard, beyond exhaustion, to prove that I am worthy or to prove to others that they made the right decision by giving me the project, the job promotion, or the salary increase.
- I charge less for my work or give discounts through my business, even before being asked. Charging market value makes me uncomfortable when I think my work may not be worth that money.
- I procrastinate on important projects, which is an unconscious way of protecting myself from making mistakes because those would confirm that I'm not great at what I do after all.

You have taken a great first step by observing how the cultural script of inferiority shows up in your life. Feeling inadequate, inferior, or second-class is a deep and silent cultural burden we do not discuss. Or rather, we did not discuss it since we are already creating change by allowing ourselves to observe with neutrality how the feeling of inferiority shows up in our lives and what behaviors it influences. Observation and awareness are a great first step towards transformation.

THE CULTURAL SCRIPT OF SILENCE

Have you ever heard the infamous «*Calladita te ves más bonita*» or «Children have nothing to say here»? Those messages, even when meant as jokes, had a real impact. They come from cultural traditions and gender roles that indicate that women and children do not have the right to express their voices in the same way that men do. Remember that in our culture, men historically dominated spaces of power and influence such as business, government, the Church, and the military. Women and children do not express their opinions in those spaces, or at least not openly.

The cultural script of silence was born not only out of systemically oppressing self-expression. In our Latino culture, silence was achieved through physical punishment: the sandal («la chancla»), the belt, and even a slap have been effective at creating respect (or at least silence) towards figures of authority in our lives. Don't we say, referring to our Generation Z children, «If I had raised my voice like that to my father, I would have already received a good "chanclazo"?»

This topic was discussed at length during our Rising Together full day of training in Boston, a movement I founded to help transform our relationship with ourselves, money, and power. As we discussed our cultural tendency to remain silent in conflict, a young woman stood up. She expressed: «Our past experiences, particularly those in which physical punishment was involved to ensure respect for authority, keep haunting us today each time we remain silent with a manager or executive at work or when we are with people of a race that we perceive as superior to ours.» Although it hurts to admit it, the «chanclazo» imposed respect for authority, but it also exacerbated our tendency towards silence and survival. We generally don't talk about this. However, I dared to bring this up during a TV interview.

I was invited to CUNYTV in New York for the «Caliente Caliente» segment some time ago. Among the various topics we touched on was physical punishment within the Latino community. While looking firmly at the camera, I remember saying, «If you find yourself in a meeting and are afraid to express your opinion, you may be going through life with a "chancla" still stuck to your head.» Beyond how funny this image may be, it represents the reality of many in our community. Many of us received a «chanclazo» or some slaps during our childhood and unconsciously repeated the pattern with our children. Unless we eradicate that cultural legacy, we will continue silencing and limiting our loved ones.

The «chanclazo» and other attempts to silence and oppress the voices of our young ones may create the opposite effect, provoking an unhealthy and counterproductive rebellion. In one of my coaching sessions, a client expressed that it was almost impossible for her to keep calm in the face of authority figures, especially if they were white men. On several occasions, she had not been able to control the words that came out of her mouth nor the energy with which she expressed them. She felt that she was destroying essential work relationships and that she was being labeled as difficult. When she shared more about her childhood, she recounted how she had to assume the role of translator and protector of her immigrant parents at a very young age, as they sought refuge in silence when faced with authority figures. In those situations, she felt such helplessness that she would have liked to scream at the top of her lungs, but feeling unsafe, she would also remain silent. She felt oppressed so many times that, over the years, she could no longer contain that girl who had not been able to express herself. The silence of her past returned as screams in her present, affecting her future and her inner peace.

In our community, seeking emotional or psychological help is stigmatized since that is seen as only for unstable people («para locos»). In my personal experience, and in that of so many Latinas who have managed to heal a painful past to create an extraordinary present, therapy has been a key and fundamental pillar, mainly because through the process, we embraced that those who silenced our voices did the best they could with what they knew at the time. If they had known how to do it better, they would possibly have done it better.

Let's explore how the cultural script of silence generally influences specific behaviors. Point out those with which you identify:

- I hide my opinions, and more so when I think that expressing them publicly might create conflict.
- I remain silent before authority figures or people different from me.
- I share my ideas once I am sure I can articulate them perfectly. I internally struggle with my fears of not being able to communicate effectively.
- I express my opinion with such force and impetus, sometimes with resentment and anger, that I damage my interpersonal relationships.
- I say «I'm sorry» or «Excuse me» too frequently or ask permission to give my opinion.

This script haunted me for decades. Too many times, I found myself struggling with my inner voices of disempowerment and self-invalidation. When I wanted to say something that could generate conflict, I waited until someone else said it first to see how the group reacted, or when I had a brilliant idea, I doubted so much about how to articulate it that I lost the opportunity when someone else presented it and received all the credit. I silenced myself again and again, as millions of us have done. Because of the cultural script of silence, we have believed that our voice does not count or that expressing ourselves can be dangerous. Later on, we will start changing this through our act of healthy rebellion.

THE CULTURAL SCRIPT OF SERVING OTHERS ABOVE ALL ELSE

During that Rising Together conference in Boston, a topic generated the most discussion and exchange of ideas: Latina women tend to say «Yes» too soon to requests we receive in our workplaces without fully understanding what we are saying yes to. Then we get home and realize we may have made a mistake by promising more than we can feasibly deliver. As a result, we end up exhausted from trying to make everyone happy except ourselves. The script of serving others above all else is very subtle, and it appears disguised as the inner pressure to accommodate the interests of others and put them above our own. In other words, it leads us to create a life without us in its center.

Ancestrally, Latina women were educated to follow the male lead and to serve the man of the house and the children, mainly playing a behind-the-scenes role that has not always been valued. Over time, and particularly in the last two generations, millions of Latina women are going out into the world, being the first in generations to access a college education and professional spaces that were not available to our mothers and grandmothers. However, our collective subconscious and unconscious do not upgrade as quickly as the pace of change in our external circumstances, so without being fully aware of it, we may continue to carry cultural mandates assigned to our gender, not fully realizing and exercising our power.

These cultural mandates have a more profound impact on us than just conditioning us to place other people first; they also influence significant decisions concerning «how much of a woman we are.» For example, they pressure us to get married before a certain age, generally before 30. Once we say yes, there is pressure to climb up to the next step of what defines our value as women: becoming mothers («When is the baby coming?»). And, once we are mothers, we face the cultural weight of being the one person in the household who carries the majority of the child-rearing and household care tasks. If we add to this already heavy load our professional obligations and aspirations, sooner or later, we will collapse under the weight of trying to be full-time professionals, mothers, and heads of household. If we don't break this cycle, years will pass and we will continue to create a life in which we are not the center.

Much of my collapse in 2016 was caused by this script. In 2007, my husband and I decided to become parents. When my daughter Valentina was born, I felt enormous inner pressure to continue my career. I had invested so much in my education and corporate career that I wanted to continue on that path. However, the cultural mandate of being the one who would take care of my children full-time presented itself with full force in such a way that I could not trust anybody else to take care of my daughter. Trying to be a full-time professional and mother, I abandoned myself to become everything to others, leading to my massive collapse.

Point out the behaviors that indicate the existence in your life of this cultural script of service to others above all else:

- I say «Yes» without being sure what I am committing to, only to later realize that I accepted a project beyond what my time and resources allow.
- I work past the point of exhaustion to fulfill all the obligations that I take on.
- I put aside what is important to me because somebody else does not see it as necessary. For example, I might fail to attend one of my children's school events because I think my superiors will get angry or change their perception of me.
- I live in a continuous dilemma, internally struggling between making others happy and making myself happy, feeling that neither is possible simultaneously.
- I feel guilty when I finally put myself first and do something for myself, no matter how small.

At our conference in Boston, the debate became even more interesting when someone in the room asked, «If we start saying "no" without overthinking about it, aren't we going to be letting go of possible growth opportunities?» Saying *yes* or *no* to an opportunity is not always an obvious decision. It is an art filled with nuances. In that art, what's most important for those who want to paint their professional future intentionally is to stop the automatic tendency to serve the interests of others above ours and, instead, ask all the necessary questions and take time to evaluate the implications before making a final decision. Make sure that your choices have you at the center of your life because if you collapse, everything around you, inside and outside the office, can collapse, too.

THE CULTURAL SCRIPT OF PERFECTIONISM

Perfectionism or, rather, an epidemic of perfectionism?

Last summer, my family took a few days off at the beach. On one of those days, when the weather was cloudy and cool, I went for a walk with my teenage daughter, and we had one of the most insightful conversations of our lives.

—Valentina, do you feel pressure being the daughter of immigrants? —I asked her very directly. With today's teenagers, you can't beat around the bush too much because they quickly lose patience.

—I don't just feel pressure. I feel I must be the perfect daughter: go to the best college to get a better job than the one you had. And if I don't achieve that, I feel I will become the disappointment of my ancestors —she told me.

At 15 years old, Valentina summed up what I had heard from hundreds of Latina women who are daughters of immigrants. They feel pressure to achieve more than what their parents achieved, and many feel the additional pressure to become their families' emotional and financial pillars.

—Tell me a little more. What do you mean by disappointing your ancestors? —I asked her.

—You and Dad arrived as immigrants with nothing. You were the first to go to college and accomplished a lot. I feel that

I must achieve even more and go for more than you. And if I don't do it, I will not only be a disappointment to you but to all my ancestors. And that, to me, means that I have to be perfect.

Valentina is well aware of our humble beginnings and of a reality in our native Argentina that is very different from hers in the U.S. However, I never imagined that at such a young age, she already felt pressure to make her parents', grandparents', and great-grandparents' sacrifices worthwhile, thinking that what they went through would have meaning and be justified only if she could achieve more than what all of us before her have accomplished. What's worse about this is her self-imposed pressure to be perfect. I know very well the consequences that pursuing perfectionism had on me, and I don't want that for my daughter.

My obsession with perfectionism started when I was seven or eight years old, every time my parents' eyes lit up with my school report card. Knowing that my academic success made them happy, I embarked on the mission of having impeccable grades. Later in life, that translated into becoming the perfect employee, now seeking not only my parents' approval but also that of my superiors.

This is how, day in and day out, I put my head down to work harder and harder to exceed the expectations of others, who rewarded my sacrifice with sporadic compliments or positive comments but rarely with a salary increase or a promotion. Instead of asking for them, I worked even harder, trying to convince myself that the salary increase or the promotion was almost there for me. Until I collapsed; my body and mind said, «Enough.»

Perfectionism is an epidemic in our community. Pursuing a model of success often established for non-Latino white people, we find ourselves climbing a mountain that seems too steep, and that makes us question ourselves and our value. When we feel that we are not progressing in our uphill climb, we rely on hard work as the only formula to move forward.

Among Latina women, the bombardment of messages that deepens our insecurities and damages our self-esteem begins at an early age. We are taught to criticize ourselves and to believe that what society considers desired or perfect is not what we are:

Don't even think about going out in the sun; you'll tan too much!
You and your lousy hair are impossible to control.
You're too fat; no man will look at you like that.
Don't move your hands so much when you talk: they're too distracting.
What do you mean you're not interested in learning to cook? No one will marry you like that.
What do you mean you don't plan to have children? Good wives give their husbands children.
Why are you crying now? How dramatic! Come on, shake it off, and move on.

Those messages expressed by authority figures, sometimes innocently to protect us, and other times directly in the form of criticism in an attempt to correct us, had a real impact on our mindsets and our behaviors.

Point out how the cultural script of perfectionism manifests in your life:

- I feel I have to be an example for others, and I carry the pressure to create something greater than what my ancestors achieved.
- I procrastinate or postpone important projects or decisions. I can feel so overwhelmed by the pursuit of perfection that I don't even know where to start, leaving the project until the last moment when there is no alternative, impacting my work's quality.
- I feel so uncomfortable with ambiguity that I only express my ideas or opinions if they are perfect.

- I continually push myself beyond exhaustion at work, even when I know that I may end up with a physical, mental, or emotional collapse.
- I reject who I am, which shows up as anxiety, depression, or even eating disorders.

Until now, I have invited you to identify the behaviors that block you the most. Why? Because I want you to become aware of them and accept them. Now, that acceptance can be compelling in transforming your life. It's not about giving up and throwing in the towel, but about being at peace with our situation, knowing that we are human and that many of our actions, thoughts, and feelings have an unconscious root. To accept is also to make peace with having made mistakes or having held thoughts or behaviors against our well-being and happiness. To accept is to learn to love our limitations and the human being we are, who did the best they could with they knew at the time.

Let's consider some acts of healthy rebellion that concern acceptance.

First, let's accept that the cultural scripts we covered were transmitted to us through generations and unconsciously by people who did the best they humanly could. What you and I know today, they did not know. If they had known, they would have acted differently. With this, we can begin to forgive them.

Second, let's accept in our hearts that the model of perfection we were programmed to achieve is so disconnected from our reality that it will simply be unattainable. Not because we are inferior but because it is a model created without considering our culture and unique needs and goals. It's a misuse of our energy to try to change who we are or how we express ourselves; it's better to invest that energy into achieving our goals. Let's accept that our personal highest potential is the only yardstick to measure our success.

Third, let's accept that it's okay not to feel okay about ourselves and about a system that doesn't fully embrace us for who we are. We don't have to pretend to be strong and perfect. Feeling uncomfortable, frustrated, tired, or occasionally powerless is okay. As individuals who are 100% responsible for our reality and destiny, let's take the necessary steps to heal what needs to be healed and forgiven.

ACT OF HEALTHY REBELLION

*Analize the behaviors you marked
in this chapter and answer:*

*What fears or beliefs do I need to accept?
How can I start living differently?*

_____
_____
_____
_____

To accept means, in short, to become fully aware of our inherited cultural scripts, let them go, and forgive others and ourselves. We can draw strength from that space of peace to start doing things differently. That is the best way to rebel.

LESSONS LEARNED

- Generation after generation, we have absorbed cultural beliefs that unconsciously impact our daily actions and decisions.

- The script of inferiority shows up when we feel inadequate or lacking. It has its roots in a system whose model of success was created without considering the cultural nuances, needs, and goals of professionals like us.

- The script of silence makes us believe that we are safer if we do not express our opinions because by speaking we can get in trouble. One of the roots of silence lies in the physical punishment we received when we questioned our parents during childhood.

- The script of service appears disguised as internal pressure to serve the interests of others and put them above our own. It has a greater impact on women, who were pushed into a behind-the-scenes role.

- The script of perfectionism arises when we are influenced to believe in a success model that seems distant from who we truly are. In response, we insist on working harder and appearing perfect to close that gap. Perfectionism can manifest as procrastinating on important projects or decisions, further driving stress and pressure.

- An important part of our transformative journey requires us to accept that those who influenced our thinking did the best they could with what they knew. The process of forgiving those authority figures and ourselves for having pushed us to act in ways that ended up wearing us down is a major key to our growth.

CHAPTER 3

Latina sisters, are we united?

I confess that this chapter and the next were challenging to write. My inner voices went off. I wondered, «Am I doing the right thing by discussing these controversial topics? It's very uncomfortable. What if someone gets offended or what I say rubs people the wrong way? I'd better leave it for tomorrow... Today is not a good day to write about this topic.»

The inner voices of doubt and fear became quite loud, even more so when I wrote a post on social media about the notorious lack of unity in the Latino cohort. That post was one of the most viewed among everything I have shared but one with the fewest reactions and comments. It was as if people were afraid to publicly admit their thoughts and feelings about what had been happening. The «We don't talk about that» keeps winning the battle.

Despite the general silence, I received several private messages from people who did not feel safe openly expressing their opinions for fear of retaliation: «Thank you for putting into words what many of us think but don't dare to say,» someone told me. «I can't speak my truth. I'm afraid of losing my job or being labeled as the problematic Latina.»

I perfectly understand. It is not easy to be an agent of change in our professional spaces, as we can find ourselves in a continuous dilemma. We are told to speak our truth without being controversial or to be more assertive and direct while keeping everyone happy. Or that we have to change the system but not make anybody uncomfortable in the process. I feel that generating substantial changes while making everyone happy during the process is impossible.

From the moment we commit to starting to change things, the process will inevitably be uncomfortable, even for ourselves. For me, it still is. And possibly it will be for you, too. So, join me as we allow ourselves to feel a bit uncomfortable, angry, or maybe relieved about the topics we will discuss next. Let's permit ourselves to let our inner voices shout out what we have suppressed for too long, and let's look into all we have swallowed to the point of indigestion.

THE ELEPHANT IN THE ROOM

«The elephant in the room» is an expression I learned when I arrived in the United States in 2002; it refers to something big and quite apparent that is denied or ignored because of the discomfort it generates. Imagine a business meeting with a dozen professionals seated around the table. In that meeting, a giant elephant is sitting in the middle of the table, as an analogy for a severe problem that is inescapable and inevitable but that no one wants to discuss. Everyone can see it, but no one dares to mention that there is an elephant in the middle of the room.

In our Latino community, the elephant in the room is our lack of unity. We are not united! Although in the United States, people refer to «Latinos» or «Hispanics» as if we were one cohesive group or community, we can be more like a dysfunctional and divided family. And that elephant that we pretend not to see and do not talk about is, in my view, one of the most perverse and silent brakes to our individual and collective progress. It is up to us to admit (without judgment, please!) that we compete with each other, envy one another, and feel tempted to block or turn our backs on another Latina who begins to move faster than us.

With this in mind, why complain about the system's unfairness when our collective behavior contributes to our situation to a certain extent? We are not victims but create our reality through actions or inaction.

Most of us are aware of this elephant in the room. In other words, we are quite aware of our reality.

An IBM Institute for Business Value survey recently asked thousands of Latinos and Latinas if they agreed that the Latino community is united and speaks with a unified voice. Only 16% of respondents answered affirmatively.

So, if we know that we are not united, do not have a common voice, and are not walking together in the same direction, why do we feel we need to stay silently looking at that elephant in the room? Why do we not dare to talk about it? I asked this same question to several leaders in our community, and here are some of the reasons they gave me for the silence we hold in the face of our lack of unity:

> *Our division is ancestral and so rooted in colonial thinking that I don't think we are fully aware of the impact it causes.*
>
> *In spaces where we don't feel entirely at home, we can be so focused on our progress that we have no time or energy to think as a group.*
>
> *Our lack of unity is so ingrained in our culture that it is utopian to think we will unite one day. Why talk about it? It will make no difference.*
>
> *We are influenced by the «Don't air your dirty laundry» or «What will people say!?» so we pretend everything is fine even if it bothers us.*

We can find a thousand reasons not to discuss this issue. Still, I am sure that from the moment you opened this book, you noticed that in this space, we confront the most controversial or uncomfortable issues that affect our community, and we do so head-on. So, let's unravel the root causes of our division, beginning with the most visible ones.

VERY DIVERSE AND QUITE LOADED WITH JUDGMENTS

I am Argentinian, and she is Mexican. We speak a little differently and even eat very different foods. I see that we have little in common.

Are Afro-Latinas Latinas? Don't they identify more with the African American community?

She is not fluent in Spanish and is not a true Latina. She doesn't even have a Latina name.

I thought you had to be born in the United States to be Latina. I am Peruvian, not Latina.

One of your parents is not Latino? Then you are not as Latina as I am. Both my parents came from Latin America. It's not the same.

She looks pretty white. More like a gringa than a Latina. Besides, everything must be easier for her.

A large part of our division stems from our profound diversity as a community: our many different countries of origin, skin colors, unique traditions and customs from our countries of origin that we still preserve, language of preference, access to education, and socioeconomic level all can contribute to highlight our differences. But fundamentally, a core reason for seeing ourselves as different from other Latinas is how we perceive our identity and our degree of belonging to Latinidad compared to them.

Let's start with our countries of origin. Although almost 60% of Latinas in the United States come from Mexico or have Mexican ancestry, the remaining 40% come from more than twenty different countries, each with a strong sense of national pride, embracing its unique culture, and presenting language variations, as the same word can mean something different depending on the country where you find yourself.

Approximately 77% of Latinas know there are many subcultures within our community and know this has to do with the many countries we originate from. Our national pride is deeply rooted among us. So much so that, despite the many failed attempts to put us all under one unique label, be it Hispanic, Latina, Latinx, Latine, or other versions of it, statistics show that half of us identify more closely with the Latin American countries our families came from (Mexican, Dominican, Cuban, Argentinian, Salvadorian, etc.) than with any of the other labels.

That connection with our countries of origin is so strong that you will have a slightly different experience of our Latinidad, depending on which city in the United States you visit. This happens because different cities have a greater or lesser influence from different Latin American countries. For instance, while 78% of Latinos in Chicago and 75% of Latinos in Los Angeles identify as Mexican, in Orlando, Florida, you find that 43% of Latinos come from Puerto Rico, and in Miami, Florida, 40% come from Cuba. If you visit Washington, DC, you will find that 31% of Latinos are Salvadorian. Consequently, each city develops a Latino subculture. It is possible for us to feel a little bit like a foreigner among our people.

Let's pause to reflect on how confusing it must be for a non-Latino individual to understand the cultural nuances within our community. That is why some companies have thrown millions of dollars down the drain trying to reach us with marketing campaigns that fail to understand us or to speak to our hearts. If companies want to continue capturing a larger share of the growing Latino market, they need us seated at the table where those strategic decisions are made. After all, we are second to none in understanding the nuances and complexities of our community.

NEITHER FROM HERE NOR FROM THERE?

We also perceive each other differently depending on our level of acculturation or adoption of American customs, traditions, and values. Some of us arrived a long time ago, others more recently, and in some cases, multiple generations of ancestors lived in this country. Thus, some Latinas can feel more from here than from there, and others more from there than from here, displaying varied confidence levels in making their way through the American system. Some of us move like fish in water, and others, as they would say in my hometown, feel like toads from another well.

Latina women are divided into three reasonably distinctive groups. Statistics show that one-third were born in a foreign country, another third were born in the United States to immigrant parents, and the remaining third have been here for several generations of ancestors. Some of these ancestors were not immigrants, but Mexican families were already on this side of the Rio Grande in 1848 when the existing border between Mexico and the United States was established.

In theory, the more time passes, the more uses and customs of the American culture we adopt, such as celebrating 4th of July or Thanksgiving, shaking hands instead of hugging people, or even maintaining a greater physical distance when communicating with others. After a decade of living in this country, I realized while visiting Argentina that when someone approached me to have a conversation and stood too close, I would take a few discreet steps back to create more distance from the person. I did it automatically, unconsciously. I had gotten used to the distance we maintain in the United States when communicating. We gradually start emulating the new culture, almost without realizing it.

If you think those who have been in this country for a longer time or more generations have it easier or feel more comfortable, let me share a conversation that shattered my views.

Myriam is a Latina woman who lives in El Paso, Texas. Her ancestors have been established «on this side of the Rio Grande» for countless generations. When I met her, I assumed she would feel like a «typical American,» with a strong sense of belonging to this culture. However, in one of our conversations, she confessed that she doesn't feel one hundred percent purely American and that sometimes she is tempted to hold back her expression when with white non-Latino men. She observed that from her mother, who showed a strong personality around other people in our Latino community but made herself smaller and kept silent in front of white non-Latino Americans.

Right there, I realized the dangers of making assumptions and generalizations. It doesn't matter if three or four generations have passed; some Latina women still don't feel entirely at home. Moreover, their children can inherit feelings of being different or even uncomfortable. Statistics indicate that many of us feel this way; according to Pew Research, 44% of Latinos and Latinas in the United States (almost half!) feel very different from a typical American. We are talking about 26 million Latinos and Latinas who feel different from «the norm.» I wonder how many of those don't feel they belong or don't feel welcome within our community because they have been judged as not Latina or Latino enough?

TELL ME WHAT LANGUAGE YOU SPEAK, AND I WILL TELL YOU WHO YOU ARE

Our language and how fluently we speak it can cause division and a source of shame and stigma. Because language is strongly connected to our expression and has ties to the culture we come from and the one we navigate in this country, we may feel enormous pressure to speak both languages perfectly.

That's how those of us who have an accent can often feel a particular shame about how we speak or put pressure and unrealistic expectations on ourselves, wishing we could pronounce words as well as someone born here. On the other hand, those who speak perfect English and have lost their command of Spanish may feel ashamed when faced with the laughter of their relatives («But look how gringa you are!») or the judgments of Latinos who speak perfect Spanish («Look at her, she wants to act white, she doesn't even speak our language anymore!»).

Language proficiency varies significantly among us. While 36% of Latinas are bilingual, 25% primarily use English to communicate, and the remaining 38% mainly use Spanish. And let's remember Portuguese, which always seems to be left out of these statistics!

When I arrived in the United States in 2002, I loaded myself with judgments towards Latinos who did not speak Spanish because «how is it possible that they haven't learned it?» Over time, and as a mother of two children born in this country, I have accepted that my children have more ease in one language or the other, and I allowed them to express themselves freely as they choose instead of interrupting them at every minute demanding a «Speak Spanish!» Other families forced their children to stop speaking Spanish to prevent them from developing an immigrant accent. This survival strategy sought to get their kids accepted in the new culture.

Over time, I stopped judging a person as more Latina or less Latina based on their language and understood that we can unite beyond the language we use to communicate.

So far, we only covered some of the intersections that make up our diversity. There are more, including our differences in access to education. In our community, there is a minority that has had access to formal education and a large majority that has not followed that path. Only 23% of Latinos between the ages of 25 and 29 have a college degree (compared to 45% of white non-Latinos). Likewise, only 3% of Latinos have a master's degree, and less than 1% have completed their doctorate. In our countries of origin, where classism predominates, it is almost unthinkable that two individuals with such radically different access to formal education would identify as belonging to the same social group. Our differences in educational levels contribute to deepening a sense of division. If we continue to hold classist points of view, we will limit the upper mobility of our younger Latinos.

Our lack of unity affects us in several ways. When we feel separated from each other, we don't transfer valuable knowledge and experiences among one another, we refrain from recommending another Latina for a job opportunity, and we don't use our social capital for the advancement of our collective. Turning our backs on other Latinas or feeling disinterested in her progress has real consequences: our cohort continues to be left behind and relatively absent from spaces of power. At the same time, we observe groups whose members support each other take the lead in front of us to get where we would love ourselves to be. We become spectators of a collective success that could have been ours but slips through our fingers. The ancestral paradigms and limiting beliefs that have not worked for us keep winning the battle.

We need each other if we want to go far. Let's not be fooled by the cultural belief that we can make it alone. We probably can, up to a certain level, but our professional progress will stall.

Our challenge as a family is to stop measuring our degree of Latinidad according to variables such as country of origin, level of acculturation, and language. Let's accept our inescapable diversity and recognize that those who have learned to swim in this system, like fish in water, have the opportunity to support the development of those who still feel like toads from another well. Just as unity strengthens us, perpetuating disunity will accelerate our collective demise.

> **ACT OF HEALTHY REBELLION**
>
> **Reflect:**
>
> *What specific action steps can
> I take today to create unity in our Latino community?*
>
> _____
> _____
> _____
> _____
> _____

We are here to reverse our tendency toward isolation, because in our unity lies the key to progress. Only through our unity in diversity and by helping one another we will cease to be a paradox of powerful women without power.

LESSONS LEARNED

- The lack of unity in our community, that elephant in the room that we pretend not to see or find hard to talk about, is possibly the most perverse brake to our individual and collective advancement.

- Much of our division originates from our diversity, such as coming from different countries of origin, skin colors, languages, socioeconomic levels, and degrees of belonging to our community.

- When we feel separated and different from each other, we tend to stop sharing knowledge, experiences, opportunities, and key connections that can help us grow.

- Consequently, we end up relegated and absent from the spaces where we should be, while other groups whose members support each other keep moving forward into those spaces.

- Accepting our inescapable diversity and sharing what is ours with other Latinas is the only weapon against our isolation and lack of significant advancement.

CHAPTER 4

Colorism: How we deny our history

Some time ago, my dear friend Carmen called me crying. The night before, she had been at a social gathering where, in front of 15 other people, a Latina friend she had known for decades blurted out:

—Carmen, why did you marry a European? To improve the race?

Everyone around the table laughed, most visibly uncomfortable, but no one said anything. Carmen, an immigrant from Venezuela, silently endured the humiliation and shame she felt with this aggression from her most intimate circle.

Colorism, or the superiority of individuals with white skin and European features, is a disease that our community has carried since colonial times. Through the eyes of colorism, Latinos and Latinas who have white skin are deemed better, more intelligent, and deserving of trust. In contrast, those in our community who have darker skin can be considered inferior, less capable, and, in some cases, even dangerous. According to Pew Research, 22% of Afro-Latinos surveyed (referring to Latinos who have some degree of African ancestry) have been unjustly detained by police, compared to only 8% of non Afro-Latinos. Other studies highlight that Afro-Latinos are viewed with suspicion when they enter a store and sometimes are even followed through the aisles.

Colorism has its origins in our diversity. The Latino community is a melting pot of races, with a mixture of Indigenous,

Black, White, and Asian blood present in each one of us to different degrees. That is why we have brown, tan, white Latinas, Afro-Latinas, Asian-Latinas, and many other intersectionalities. In this wide variety, those who suffer racism the most are undoubtedly Afro-Latinas.

According to the same Pew Research report, in 2020, there were around 6 million Afro-Latino adults in the United States, representing approximately 2% of the adult population and 12% of the adult Latino population. Afro-Latino men and women have been significantly and historically relegated and discriminated against, not only in the United States but throughout Latin America.

In my process of discovering our past, the one that history books tried to hide from us, I learned that during the colonial period, approximately 15 times more enslaved Africans were taken to the Spanish and Portuguese colonies than to the United States. Therefore, around 130 million people of African descent live in Latin America today, representing approximately 25% of the total population of that region. One out of four! It makes me wonder how it can be possible that, except for a few exceptions, their contributions have not been fully recognized. Moreover, how many Afro-Latinos and Afro-Latinas are in spaces of power and influence in Latin America, such as corporations, government, or the media? Very similar to what happens to us in the Latino community in the United States, in Latin America Afro-Latinos and Afro-Latinas are relatively absent from leadership, power and decision-making spaces.

Not fully acknowledging the importance and influence of the Afro-Latino community in our collective history is equivalent to ignoring our past, and this denial of an essential part of who we are as a community perpetuates painful experiences, such as the one my friend Carmen went through.

In my author journey, it has been quite painful to listen to the stories of my Afro-Latina friends: women I had known for decades, or rather women whose stories I thought I knew until they gathered the courage to share with me all those painful experiences they silently carried most of their lives: discrimination, prejudice, and aggression perpetrated by other Latinos and Latinas and even by some of their family members. They were subject to words that were perhaps accepted in the past but that today can make our skin crawl: *Get out of the sun, or you'll get darker! Look how beautiful that baby is, so fair-skinned! You can't go to the street with that lousy hair (ese pelo malo)!*

Listening to their stories has been one of the most eye-opening and saddest experiences I have had in recent years. It allowed me to see a reality I was unaware of simply because I was born with lighter skin. I learned that an essential part of our collective history had been suppressed for centuries, causing real damage to our people.

COLORISM HAS REAL AND PERVERSE CONSEQUENCES

In a Pew Research study, a majority (62%) of Latino adults surveyed expressed that having a darker skin color limits professional advancement in the United States. Nearly six out of ten (61%) of Afro-Latinos surveyed said they had experienced at least one incident of discrimination in the last year, compared to 54% of Latinos without African ancestry. Additionally, 35% of Afro-Latinos included in the survey said another Latino had discriminated against them. Someone from our community!

Receiving negative comments about their physical features, being forced to sit at the back of the class because their intellectual ability was questioned, not being invited to events or conferences because «they don't belong here,» not being recognized in the media, magazines, or awarded; being excluded from boards of directors, are just a few of the ways in which Afro-Latinas continue to suffer the denial of their capabilities and contributions, which is a type of violence and discrimination.

When found in spaces of power and visibility, they encounter silent judgments (*Did she get here because of her skin color? Did the organization check a box with her?*), which unfairly cast doubt on their experience and merit. A study by the University of California, Los Angeles, challenges this prejudice by showing how Afro-Latina women have achieved higher levels of education than other Latina women in our community: 26% have completed college, compared to 18% for the rest of our Latinas.

—These experiences made me feel my identity is denied as if my blood and my ancestors were something to be ashamed of —Carmen confessed—. The worst part is that I think I can't say anything about it because I don't want to be judged as a problematic woman of color.

Like so many other Afro-Latina women, Carmen told me that sometimes she doesn't feel like part of the Latino community nor a member of the African American community. For Afro-Latina women, the effects of oppression and discrimination are so profound and devastating that they can end up impacting their identity, self-worth, and self-esteem.

The last census is eye-opening in this regard, as three out of ten Afro-Latinos and Afro-Latinas self-identify as belonging to the white race. It took me a long time and several conversations with Afro-Latina friends to understand the reason for that self-identification. These women explained to me that associating with the dominant group that has historically risen in all spaces of power can be a survival mechanism for some members of the Afro-Latino community. Imagine the degree of oppression and discrimination that this community has faced to reach that point.

The impact on identity is reflected not only in statistics but also in everyday life events. As Dr. Marisol Capellán expresses in her revealing book «Leadership is a Responsibility,» Afro-Latina women are not only expected to act like men to succeed, they also have to act «whiter.» They modify their way of dressing, their hair, and even how they speak to be perceived as «less ethnic» or to not «make those we have in front of us feel uncomfortable.» With this, they try to be accepted to access opportunities and job promotions, or they seek to be listened to or at least less interrupted when they speak up in a meeting.

I hope this information has been as enlightening for you as it has been for me and that it invites you to reflect on the oppression experienced by a large sector of our community and on the relative privilege of those of us with lighter skin. But we cannot end like this. Let's explore how we can use our privilege, even if it seems small, for the benefit of our community. This is where I would like to share more about my personal story with you.

BEING A WHITE-SKINNED LATINA IN THE UNITED STATES

I will speak to you from my heart about something I had never dared to mention publicly for fear of being judged as insensitive or inconsiderate. Despite how uncomfortable this is, I feel I need to express what it has meant for me to be a white Latina woman in the United States, perhaps speaking up as my act of healthy rebellion. Let's explore together what it means to have a proud Latina heart and, at the same time, live in a physical body that looks like that of a non-Latina white American woman.

Since I arrived in the United States, there have been times I did not feel entirely accepted by my Latino community nor by non-Latino white Americans. I experienced what it is to feel you don't wholly belong to either group, although what hurt the most was to be considered almost an outsider by my own Latino family. After leaving my corporate career, I pursued my calling to support the self-empowerment and growth of our community, giving back from all I received in my life. That calling has been so clear that those times I did not feel accepted in our community hurt quite a lot. For example, I was a panelist at an in-person event in the Latino community a few months ago. Half an hour before the panel started, I met with the other panelists in a room adjacent to the conference room to agree on the final details before going on stage. In that meeting, there was a man and three other Latina women.

I arrived at the room early, feeling a little nervous, as I usually feel when speaking in public, and I sat down to wait for my fellow panelists to arrive. When one of the other Latina women arrived, I noticed she kept her distance when we greeted each other in English. However, that tension diminished after hugging her and introducing myself in Spanish. The experience with the second Latina woman was different, though. As we went around the table introducing ourselves, I noticed that she wasn't looking at me in the eyes. I tried to break the ice by asking her a question, but she responded with her eyes fixed on the other panelists without looking at me. Those tiny gestures make a big difference and make me wonder if I really belong to this community. They create distance from people who incorrectly assume that I am not Latina or who draw conclusions about my identity, origin and language based on my physical appearance alone.

After I stepped out of my corporate career in 2016, I was asked to lead an incubator for Hispanic small businesses. One evening, I had the opportunity to introduce myself to 250 people to discuss the incubator's initiatives for the coming year. With my heart beating fast in front of that crowd, I took the microphone and greeted them with an effusive «¡Buenas noches!» (Good evening!) in my native Spanish. I quickly noticed the looks of surprise and confusion. Some people in the audience discreetly leaned toward the person next to them, murmuring something while their eyes remained fixed on me. Well, that was uncomfortable! I could almost read their thoughts, «Is she Latina or Gringa?» they would ask themselves in confusion. «Look at how she looks, she's Gringa. But she speaks Spanish so well!» My mind imagined the entire scene in a few seconds.

At the end of my presentation, I would confirm what I had sensed. As people approached me to ask questions or say hello, some asked, «How is it possible that an American woman like you learned to speak Spanish so well?»

Through those experiences, I realized, perhaps for the first time, that how I look makes some people think I can't be Latina. While in our community we complain that others may have biases towards us, we also can have prejudices about how a Latina woman should or should not look. More than once, I wished I could change how I looked to feel a little more accepted. Still, over time, I learned to laugh at how ironic God has been in giving me this heart that is profoundly and proudly Latino while placing me in a package that looks whiter than white Americans. I am only one of the many examples of the incredible variety of races that make up our community.

These personal experiences led me to reflect on the impact of skin color in our community. If I had my hurdles and struggles, can you imagine the barriers that our Afro-Latinas have to face? If I feel this way, can you imagine how Afro-Latinas feel, having faced discrimination and systemic racism since they were little? We all have our obstacles, and each of us has been wounded in different ways, but we can't remain stuck in our pain and miss the opportunity to use our privilege, however small, for the benefit of others around us.

Over time, I became fully aware that this body I inhabit gives me access to spaces where I face one less barrier or where I manage to make people less uncomfortable, as Marisol Capellán would say, because of the way I look. Despite the many obstacles and struggles I had to go through as an immigrant, when I became aware of my privilege the question that arose from my heart went from «Why does everything seem so difficult for me?» to «How can I use my privilege to support our community?».

YOUR PRIVILEGE IS MEANT TO BE USED

Everybody goes through struggles and difficulties, which have probably been very tough for many of us. Personally, and because of my accent, I often had to prove that I was intelligent, no matter how many academic degrees I accumulated or how many renowned corporations I worked for. I was taken for granted, my value was questioned, and I was discriminated against for being a woman and an immigrant. Too many times, I knocked on doors that never opened, which led me to feel like a victim of a cruel system. I complained and lamented about my circumstances until I immersed myself, as I shared before, in other women's experiences.

Privilege is not an all-or-nothing proposition. It's not that we are always privileged or never are; instead, our degree of privilege varies depending on who we are surrounded with. For example, if I am around high-school age Latino children, I have an apparent privilege which is my access to a graduate education. I can use that privilege to invite them to pursue their dreams and guide them to apply to college. On the other hand, if I plan to go to a conference where the only person I'll know is a well-connected Latina executive, maybe she can use her privilege to connect me with other decision-makers. What matters is that at every moment, we ask ourselves how we can use our privilege to support others. How can we contribute a grain of sand from our spaces to break the colonial chains of racism? Because let's be frank: we are done with racial prejudice and all the division created based on the colors of our skin. This only keeps us relegated! You and I, here and now, have the opportunity to eradicate those ancestral racist habits that no one has dared to change entirely.

> **ACT OF HEALTHY REBELLION**
>
> **Answer:**
>
> *Today, how can I support another Latina woman, especially an Afro-Latina?*
>
> _____
>
> _____
>
> _____
>
> _____
>
> **I'll give you some ideas:** You can nominate her for a job opportunity or promotion, for that award she deserves so much, for her to be invited to speak at a conference or interviewed in that Latina magazine she loves. You can refer a client to her business, support her posts on social media, buy her products or services, and leave a positive review online. Another excellent way is to ask her: «What can I do for you?» not as her savior, but as equals. Let her guide you with her response, and if you want to go a step further, ask her to share her story with you.

Let's dare to break the ancestral chains of colorism once and for all. Let's participate actively in an unprecedented transformation necessary for our community and become role models of unconditional acceptance so that others can see what is possible.

COLORISM AND RACISM
ARE CLOSER THAN YOU THINK

When I was about to finish writing the previous section, my Puerto Rican friend Victoria called me on the phone. After I shared with her what I had been writing about she told me for the first time in five years of friendship that although her complexion is white, her hair is very curly.

—What?! —I asked her in amazement—. How come I have never seen your natural hair, not even last year when I stayed at your house?

Honestly, I never cease to be surprised when these things happen.

—My friend —she said to me—, I work for a corporation and must look professional. That's why I straighten my hair every day, without exception.

She told me that one of her grandmothers was Afro-Latina and that she had inherited her curly hair from her.

—When I was little, every time my hair reached my shoulders, my dad would take me to the salon to cut it very short, as if I were a boy. Back then I started to believe that my hair was ugly and that I was ugly for having that lousy hair (*pelo malo*), as my dad would call it.

That conversation left me thinking how many of us usually feel too much or not enough, but we rarely feel perfect about who we are, just as we are. We are too dark or too white, our hair looks unprofessional, or we have wide hips or a nose and lips that make us look unattractive in the eyes of a standard created without us in mind. We all have something that makes us feel unaccepted and unwelcome. Changing that feeling is up to us. We must fully accept and welcome who we are.

When saying goodbye and hanging up, I asked Victoria to send me a photo of herself with her natural, curly hair. Actually, I begged her to. She told me that she didn't have any on her cell phone since the last one she had taken was from when cell phones did not have cameras.

    She never sent me that photo, even when I insisted several times. Perhaps I was inviting her to look back into an important part of her history or essence that had caused pain, so I decided to let it go. I understood that no matter how hard I tried, I would not fully comprehend Victoria's life experiences despite loving her like a sister. It's simply not possible. What is possible is to love and value her for who she is, exactly as she is, without her feeling that she needs to change anything. As Latina women who seek to do things differently, we can give each other more unconditional acceptance and love.

LESSONS LEARNED

- Colorism, or the superiority of individuals with white skin and European features, is a disease that we have carried since colonial times.

- Afro-Latino men and women represent a large and historically relegated and discriminated group both in the United States and in Latin America. Not recognizing their importance and influence in our collective history is equivalent to ignoring our past.

- Colorism has real consequences: it limits our professional progress, exposes us to prejudices, hurtful comments, and exclusion, and affects our sense of identity and belonging.

- White Latina women can also feel that they do not fully belong to the Latino community. Addressing this topic can be uncomfortable, as they do not want to be perceived as insensitive or inconsiderate.

- Privilege is not an all-or-nothing proposition; it varies depending on who is around you.

CHAPTER 5

Relegated and fighting for crumbs

In this chapter, we will finish unmasking the elephant in the room: our classism, machismo, and tendency to compete with other Latinas, behaviors that can lead us to fight for crumbs while others eat the pie.

We may have brought these behaviors from Latin America and continue to pass them down through generations. They are ancestral and colonial, buried in our collective unconscious, from where they influence our thoughts and actions.

CLASSISM: THE CASTE SYSTEM THAT KEEPS HOLDING US BACK

Classism is the discrimination of others based on their social class. Its remote origins go back to colonial times when we were sorted into castes according to our skin color, education attainment, wealth, and mostly according to which powerful and influential people made up our social circle.

Centuries later, we continue to perpetuate this behavior. Those who belong to these select circles want to ensure that they remain in them, and it's possible that, as a survival tactic, those who do not yet belong are desperate to join. Why survival? Think of our ancestors. With limited resources and a tangible fate of remaining in poverty, receiving attention and favors from those with the power to open doors could make the difference between going to bed hungry or after a good dinner. In the colonies, belonging to those select circles provided a certain level of safety.

It is interesting to observe what can happen when we combine our ancestral classism with our scarcity mindset, which led us to believe that there are limited opportunities or no room for everybody in those exclusive circles. It's possible that once we get into those elitist spaces, we close the door behind us, excluding others from our community who are making their way in. Those of us who have once been excluded know this behavior quite well, and those who have excluded or continue to exclude may not even be aware of it.

Classist exclusion can show up in subtle behaviors, such as attending events and surrounding ourselves only with people from our same social circle, jealously guarding our contacts without sharing them with other Latinas who could benefit from them, and ignoring (or ghosting) Latinas who ask for help and do not yet have the same power and influence as we do.

This behavior can perpetuate the caste system, and what seems like a win for an individual or a small group in our community becomes a significant loss for thousands of Latina women who are left out, regardless of their talents or genuine interest in seeking support to expand their impact. I know too many talented and qualified Latinas committed to our collective advancement who end up shrinking their impact to a fraction of what would be possible due to being ignored or excluded by those with greater access and connections.

In those cases, we all lose and don't even realize it. At this time, hundreds of thousands of Latina women whom the classist system would classify as born in lower social strata are making their way at great speed in educational spaces. According to the National Center for Education Statistics, 40% of Latinas pursuing higher education degrees are the first in their family to reach that space. And if you have been the first in your family to go to college, like me, you know pretty well that graduating and having a degree does not come with the network of connections and influences that we will need to succeed professionally. Part of our transformation and success as a community will depend on providing these young Latinas with the support, mentoring, and access they need to succeed. If we don't, we will be perpetuating the colonial, classist system, where only certain privileged groups can access more privilege.

Another type of classism, perhaps more subtle than the one we discussed, seems to assign greater professional value to Latina women employed by large corporations than those who own small businesses.

—I feel awful —Dolores told me as she shared her experience at a recent Latino conference she attended. A Central American immigrant and small business owner, she had been invited for the first time to a conference where most attendees were Latinos employed by corporations or leaders of non-profit organizations. She saw it as an opportunity to expand her network of contacts, something she had been working on for years—. I felt a little out of place, not too welcome —she confessed—. I judged myself for not doing more to connect with others and for feeling inferior. I left feeling that I had done something wrong or that what I had to offer was unimportant —she confided, anguished.

A conference for Latinos in executive spaces I had attended some time ago came to mind, as I had experienced a similar feeling. In that space, the behavior dynamics of our community were worthy of observation. Those who worked in corporate spaces clearly received preferential treatment: more people approached them, conversations lasted longer, and business cards were exchanged. On the other hand, when I approached the same people without a big name on my business card but as a small business owner, I noticed that the conversation was friendly but short-lived. Some people even looked over my shoulder as I spoke to them as if scanning the room to see who else they could connect with when they were done with me.

It got to the point that when I offered my business card to that same person who had handed out their own just two seconds before, they told me they had run out of cards but would contact me soon. That contact never materialized.

I worked for almost two decades in corporate spaces at renowned global companies such as Procter & Gamble, Citibank, and McKinsey & Co. before launching my own business, so I noticed the significant difference between the treatment I received when I worked as a corporate employee and the one received when I became an entrepreneur. It is as if those who carry a renowned company on their business card belong to a higher caste than small business owners. I also unconsciously put corporate professionals on a pedestal, placing myself several rungs below.

Like Dolores, I judged myself and thought that maybe I was doing something wrong. *Is it that I'm saying something out of place? Is it that they notice I'm nervous while networking? Is it that what I have to offer is not interesting or marketable? Is it that I made a mistake and should have stayed in my corporate career?* For years, I anguished and tortured myself to the point that my head seemed to be about to explode from trying so hard to decipher what I was doing wrong. Then, talking with other Latina entrepreneurs, I learned that I am not alone and that this behavior is as systemic as it is unconscious.

Breaking away from this classist behavior can bring us great dividends. As I mentioned before, we Latinas are highly entrepreneurial. In the United States, two million businesses are created by Latina women, contributing 175 billion dollars to the country's economy. Around 90% of these firms have no employees, meaning they are micro-businesses. There is a significant and untapped economic opportunity if corporations, governments, and other large organizations extend more contracts to qualified micro-entrepreneurs and accompany them in their growth.

In recent years, companies have become more intentional about purchasing goods and services from diverse entrepreneurs, but the numbers remain low. A report by Supplier IO indicates that only 3% of purchases from surveyed companies were sourced from minority-owned businesses. And of that, only a fraction was assigned to Latina entrepreneurs. I wonder what percentage of this supplier diversity gap is systemic and how much of it occurs due to the lack of interest and support from Latinos and Latinas working in corporate spaces and similar large organizations towards female entrepreneurs qualified to deliver their goods and services, just as it happened to Dolores and myself at those conferences. Do we believe that what Latina entrepreneurs offer may not be up to par with what entrepreneurs from other communities do? Perhaps we believe their work carries a lower market value or that it is not as reliable as what a non-Latino white man offers.

As agents of change, we must deliberately break away from these ancestral paradigms and better support each other. And there is more, since Latina women not only encounter subtle forms of classism but also deal with ancestral machismo, which we will discuss next.

MACHISMO CASTS DOUBT ON LATINA WOMEN'S CAPABILITIES

Some time ago, somebody shared with me a riddle that went viral; maybe you have heard about it:

> A father and his son are traveling by car and have a severe accident. The father dies, and the son is rushed to the hospital in need of a complex emergency surgery, for which a very well-known surgeon is summoned. When this eminence enters the operating

room, they say: «I cannot operate on him; he is my son.» How can this be explained?

If you want to solve it alone, don't keep reading, as I will give you a spoiler.

The renowned surgeon is the child's mother. If you couldn't figure that out, don't feel bad. Not everyone gets to the correct answer since our brains are wired to represent the idea of a medical eminence as male. Our culture, the media, and even the books we have read lead us to think in a *machista* way.

Machismo is the attitude or way of thinking of those who maintain that men are naturally superior to women. Our Latino culture has delineated gender roles that have survived through centuries, representing men as those who dominate, protect, and provide. At the same time, women have been ancestrally defined as those who care, serve, and sacrifice for the family.

Machismo is not only bound to the idea of superiority or dominance of men in specific spaces and for certain tasks, but it can also lead to violence, aggression, and other destructive behaviors towards women and members of the LGBTQIA+ community. Machismo can also prevent men from enjoying healthy relationships in their personal lives and at work.

—Next time, you must ask me before making a decision —Raúl told a Latina woman, whom I will call Rocío, after summoning her to the conference room to meet with him privately—. You have no idea what you're doing! —he snapped at her.

Rocío has been the Logistics director for a private company for five years. Born in Venezuela and living in the United States for over two decades, she forged her career through hard work, commitment, and remarkable results. Raúl joined the company as Plant manager just a year ago. Although Raúl and Rocío are peers working at a similar seniority level, Raúl wasted no time in trying to exert his dominance over Rocío.

That was not the only controversial incident.

Three days later, Raúl stood behind Rocío while she was working at her computer in her cubicle, and he began to shout at the top of his lungs: «You're not going to disrespect me! You're going to do what I tell you!»

Rocío couldn't believe what she was hearing. In a conservative environment like that office in New Jersey, hearing a Latino colleague shouting in Spanish and trying to shame and intimidate her was more than what Rocío thought she could bear. Shockingly, no one came to her defense; her co-workers kept staring at their screens as if nothing was happening. They surely didn't understand Raúl's words, but the tone was abusive. Fed up with enduring these situations in silence, Rocío went to Human Resources that day to present her case.

—You may have misunderstood his intention —the Human Resources director said—. Raúl is driven and wants to move projects forward without significant setbacks. I understand he can be a bit temperamental sometimes, but he's a highly valued leader in this company —despite the look of disbelief on Rocío's face, he concluded—: He may have wanted to be persuasive. Maybe you're taking it too personally.

Machismo always finds a friend to defend him, particularly when a woman tries to set boundaries or speaks up against unacceptable behavior. In Raúl's case, I think his attitude was perhaps a defense mechanism for feeling inadequate and insecure in his new job or for the «shame» of sitting at the same hierarchical level as a woman.

Our community can be pretty machista, which is understandable when, in Latin America's most traditional spaces of power (such as government, the military, the Church, and agricultural spaces), women have found ourselves absent or relegated to a secondary role. Only in more recent generations have Latina women accessed college education and professional jobs outside of the home in mass numbers. Many of us have observed how our grandmothers and even our mothers assumed the role of supporting the man of the house, rather than pursuing a career or earning a living. Many men have grown up observing those same roles, so it is not entirely surprising that in their subconscious, women are equipped to assume specific roles but not others.

It is also possible that some Latina mothers exacerbate the problem (I know I have), assigning our daughters tasks that we would not assign to our sons or creating in our daughters the idea that they should depend on a man for their financial and physical safety: *When you get home, please prepare something to eat for your older brother; If you don't learn to control your temper, who will want to marry you?; How dramatic!, or Almost 30 years old and no boyfriend yet? You're going to end up single! If that happens, how will you manage?*

Many of us, to a certain extent, have heard these messages that arise from marianismo, the ideology that women should sacrifice themselves to serve others, following in the footsteps of the Virgin Mary (hence its name). Both *machismo* and *marianismo* assign specific roles and behaviors to men and women, perpetuating a system of inequity that oppresses women who wish to pursue their dreams.

In recent years, when involved with chambers of commerce and entrepreneurial spaces, I have witnessed how some Latino men tend to favor other Latino men, sharing access to their contacts and referring them to potential clients, while Latina women (some possibly more qualified) may not receive that same support, except in rare exceptions.

The good news is that the world is changing. A study by Professor Emerita Alice Eagly published by the American Psychological Association indicates that the negative perception of women's intellectual capabilities has significantly changed in recent decades. In 1946, only 35% of respondents believed that men and women were equally intelligent, while the rest considered men more intelligent than women. In 2018, 86% thought that men and women are equally intelligent. We are making progress! But what would these numbers look like if the survey were done only for the Latino community?

Our opportunity for collective growth is found in giving Latina women the space they deserve, supporting them in achieving their goals and breaking the chain to stop reinforcing *machismo* and *marianismo* thinking in younger generations, particularly those of us who are mothers. If we do so, our daughters will dare to dream that they too can become eminences in their field, like the surgeon in the riddle. As we will see later, men must be our key partners to create sustainable and scalable systemic change. The profound change process ahead of us invites us all to work together as equals.

COMPETITION AND ENVY AMONG US

Did you know that if you place several crabs inside a bucket, it's very likely that none will escape? When a crab starts climbing up, those underneath pull it down to prevent its escape. This behavior guarantees collective failure; in the end, none get out alive. It's a behavior that has been observed in the Latino community: when one of us advances and starts to succeed, it's possible that other Latinas and Latinos feel uncomfortable and, therefore, stop supporting her.

After interviewing hundreds of Latina women, I learned that this behavior is no longer novel in our community, nor does it surprise us, yet we keep repeating it! We continue pulling each other down, feeling envy and jealousy towards the one climbing up the bucket. Our unconscious can be very powerful. And although the feeling that there is not enough for everybody emanates from an ancestral way of thinking, I believe there's something even deeper. Take social media as an example. Our feeds can trigger feelings of jealousy and envy since people usually show only one part of their lives: the successful part. They don't show the sweat and tears shed along the way, nor the sacrifices and frustrations met through the process.

I'm sure this happened to you, as it did to me. Looking at what others post on social media, I have felt jealous and activated judgments towards myself for not feeling as good or successful as others. Observing these feelings, I learned that my envy concealed a reality: I yearned for that same success or recognition, but a part of me didn't believe that was possible in my life. Envy and jealousy hid my lack of self-confidence.

Since I realized this, I have done my best to stay centered when I feel jealous or envious. I focus on changing my inner dialogue and tell myself, «If she can do it, I can too.» To this thought, I add an external action, such as publicly engaging with that person's content on social media or sending them a message of support. This action allows me to trust in the universe's abundance. I trust that there is enough for everyone!

And you, how will you break through the harmful habit of pulling each other down or letting yourself be carried away by jealousy or envy?

BE THE CHANGE BY BUILDING YOUR LEGACY

Pretending that problems don't exist has a clear consequence: everything stays the same. While colorism, classism and machismo will not change overnight, touching on these issues by putting aside guilt and shame is a first step to becoming aware of how we hold back our own progress and to continue to break our chains of collective limitation. Then, an even more critical second step is necessary, which involves recognizing our relative privilege and taking a specific action (our act of healthy rebellion!). Just as we did with colorism, let's talk about privilege. Remember that privilege is relative and will vary depending on the person in front of you.

> **ACT OF HEALTHY REBELLION**
>
> *Think about five Latina women who are in your life and write:*
>
> What privileges do I have compared to each woman, and how can I use those privileges to support them?
>
> _____
>
> _____
>
> _____
>
> _____
>
> _____

Using your privilege to advance our community will give the difficulties and struggles you faced a new transcendental meaning. Your challenging experiences will no longer have taken place just for you, but they can be used to shed light for others, becoming a path to build your legacy. In this way, we can transform ourselves into giants on whose shoulders the most disadvantaged can stand to take their leap.

LESSONS LEARNED

- Classism, machismo, and the tendency to compete with other Latinas are ancestral and colonial behaviors harbored in our collective unconscious that leave us fighting for crumbs while others eat the pie.

- Classism is the discrimination of others based on their social class. Often, it involves allocating time, resources, and opportunities only to people from our social circle or a higher one, unconsciously or deliberately ignoring and excluding other Latinas who do not yet have that power or influence.

- Machismo asserts that men are naturally superior to women and assigns them the role of dominating, protecting, and providing while placing women in the role of caring, serving, and sacrificing for the family.

- Competition and a scarcity mindset lead us to behave like crabs in a bucket, pulling down those who start to rise. This survival mechanism results in envy and a failure to support the growth of other Latinas.

- You hold the keys to change: your experience with classism, machismo, and competition can be used to build a legacy if you use it to support those most affected by such behaviors.

PART II

Understand the Rules

CHAPTER 6

Change starts within you

I hope this chapter supports you in generating a lasting and profound transformation in your life. I invite you to read it carefully, mark it with colors, take notes, do the exercises, and dare to take action through the proposed acts of healthy rebellion. The most profound transformation of your life begins within you, as does the unlearning of conscious and unconscious beliefs we have held for generations. In other words, your prosperity, fulfillment, and happiness do not depend on your boss, your co-workers, your friends, or the current government. The keys to change are found within you.

Isn't it wonderful? Can you accept the possibility that the most profound change in your life can begin with yourself? It doesn't depend on anyone else. I can imagine what you might be thinking right now: *But, Valeria, in my profession, I continually face microaggressions and envy; besides, I feel that they are not paying me my market value. It seems that I should instead start to change others' ways of seeing and valuing me.*

Exactly therein lies the problem. The world has taught us a formula for change in our lives, but it was backwards. We have been handed a map where north is south and south is north. So it is easy to get lost along the way and not achieve the transformation we long for, until the day we decide to do it the other way around.

Let's explore Sara's story. An immigrant who worked as a director at a renowned financial institution for several years felt her career was slowing down. They no longer assigned her the most exciting projects, her opinions and ideas were not considered, and she even stopped being on the radar of her organization's leaders, thus losing access to their mentoring and sponsorship. At one point, her career came to an almost complete halt.

The formula for generating change that Sara had been using was:

Results → Behaviors → Inner Reality

Sara wanted to feel valued, respected and heard (inner reality), but to achieve this, she focused on first modifying her external reality (results). She thought that perhaps when a vital project was assigned to her, her leaders would take her into account and give her a promotion (results). With the support and sponsorship of those executives, she could then behave with the confidence of a leader (behavior). Consequently, others would begin listening to her, and she would feel valued and respected (inner reality).

This formula did not work. Focused on obtaining that big project, she requested meetings with her company's executives to discuss her future. However, whenever she started articulating her thoughts, her voice trembled, she felt too exposed and vulnerable, and her inner critic screamed, «What are you doing? Shut up!» The emotional and physical exhaustion was so brutal that after a decade of working in the company, she decided to find another job to change scenery. That change of environment led her to reflect on how she could do things differently, strengthening her confidence and believing in her value instead of waiting for others to validate her or highlight her contributions. Almost without noticing it, she reversed her formula to:

Inner Reality → Behaviors → Results

That's when everything changed.

—I convinced myself that I had much value to contribute —Sara told me that morning when we met for coffee and I asked her to share her story with me—. I showed up to the new job with so much self-confidence that I felt I was carrying a different energy. And others noticed it. They listened to me and gave me their full attention during meetings, and soon after they came to my office to ask about my point of view on projects they were working on.

Extraordinary results followed soon after. In a short timeframe, Sara's professional growth exponentially took off, and she became one of the few Latinas to access an executive position in the financial services industry on highly competitive Wall Street.

What Sara had done was change her internal reality (self-confidence and self-recognition of her worth), which in turn influenced how she showed up and acted daily: she now expressed herself with confidence and firmness, in a very different version of herself than the one she had shown for decades (behavior), which translated into opportunities for exponential growth, promotions, and salary increases. In other words, Sara changed her external reality because she first changed her inner world and her image of herself.

—It was really helpful to take the time I needed to reflect and observe how others I admired acted and showed up —she shared.— I noticed that others were more benevolent and less critical of themselves. For example, I remember a man with a thick accent, even more marked than mine. While I judged my immigrant accent and tortured myself, thinking that others could not understand what I said, this man's career continued to grow, accent and all, because he showed confidence in himself. That is when I realized I was getting in my way, so I decided to believe in myself and stop feeling less than others. At the end of the day, if I don't believe in myself, how can I expect others to do it?

It took Sara a few months to make that inner click; it took me many years. Those who most recently came into my life say they see in me someone who speaks in public with ease and confidence. Still, those who have known me for years and saw me in those corporate spaces, mortified and blushing every time I had to speak up, realize the hard work I had to do to transform the limited image of myself that I had been holding in my mind.

Sara and I have something in common: We learned that the first step of any profound change is pivoting our internal reality so that new behaviors flow naturally from a space of self-love and self-worth. In turn, those behaviors give rise to new results that seemed unthinkable just a few years ago. In other words, those results are nothing more than a mirror of our inner reality. So, let's step into this chapter's first act of healthy rebellion.

Do you want to change your life? Do you want to earn others' respect? Do you want to charge market value for your work? Then, stop trying to change others and focus on changing your inner world.

THREE PILLARS TO TRANSFORM YOUR INNER WORLD

Several research reports indicate the existence of a connection between our internal and external realities. An article in *Psychology Today* by Dr. Jennice Vilhauer explains that we begin to create our reality in how we perceive, interpret, and think about the events of our lives and how we respond with specific behaviors to similar situations. If you think you are a failure, you will feel like a failure; if you feel like a failure, you will behave as such.

This same article mentions that one thought constantly repeated in our minds transforms into our truth and becomes a belief. If you think you are not good at what you do and act as if that were true, you will only reinforce your belief that you are not good enough. You will then find yourself in a repetitive cycle difficult to break unless you start at the root cause: the thoughts you allow in your mind.

It is fascinating what neuroscience teaches us about the functioning of our brain. Our brains possess a mechanism called *selective filtering system*. Once a belief is established, our brain seeks to simplify stimuli from the world around us. Influenced by our beliefs, it starts scanning for specific information and blocks or inhibits the neural networks that compete with existing beliefs. In other words, our brains will favor proof that reinforces our beliefs and tend to bypass evidence to the contrary. For example, if you made the decision, even if unconsciously, that you are not good enough at what you do, your mind will have a hard time identifying and highlighting your achievements and success stories. It may overlook them.

There is something even more interesting. According to Fred Luskin, a researcher at the prestigious Stanford University, humans have around 60,000 thoughts daily, 90% of which are repetitive. In other words, we literally have a broken record in our head that obsessively thinks the same thing day after day, week after week. Hence, it is vital to become aware of what goes through our mind to break that automatic habit and pivot from limiting thoughts into expansive ones. Reprogramming our minds is possible and requires focus, effort, and repetition. This is a well-known technique among high-performance athletes. Those of us seeking the same performance level in our professions would benefit from incorporating it.

My son Tommy experienced anxiety every time he was about to play a soccer game. He thought he would play badly, lose the ball, not perform at his maximum level, and disappoint his teammates and coach. In light of that, I decided to test this concept with him. Whenever Tommy said he felt nervous and anxious before a match, I asked him to visualize himself playing like Lionel Messi, the best player in history (here's my Argentine heart showing through!). I also asked him to allow himself to feel what Messi may feel when scoring one of those almost impossible goals. And so he did. Using his imagination, he visualized himself scoring goals, allowed himself to experience a feeling of triumph even before entering the field, and changed his internal dialogue to «Yes, I can.» The results were almost immediate. His confidence increased to such an extent that in the final of a regional tournament, being one of the physically smallest players on the entire field (which in U.S. soccer is considered a disadvantage), Tommy scored two goals that allowed his team to lift the championship trophy.

With this example, please note the three fundamental components of internal transformation: 1) the images you hold in your mind, 2) the feelings accompanying those images, and 3) the inner dialogue you maintain within yourself. Let's discuss each of them.

The images you hold in your mind

Do you visualize yourself as a successful person? Can you imagine yourself acting confidently in challenging situations? It would be best if you always won in your imagination. When choosing which images of yourself to keep in your mind, lean towards positive and triumphant images, not catastrophic ones. At the beginning of this book, I promised to help you transform your thinking. Well, the first big step will be to change the way you think about yourself.

Let me share my experience. When I decided to challenge my fears and limits and launch myself as a speaker, I used my imagination to visualize myself in a desired situation. I already mentioned that in my corporate past, I used to remain silent in meetings and terrified of speaking up. So, I started creating in my mind a reality that I wanted in my life, but that, at the time, did not exist. I imagined myself in front of hundreds of people, expressing myself easily and confidently, smiling and capturing their interest. I created these visualizations with all the details, including the color and texture of the floor, the clothes we were wearing (both the people in the audience and myself), the lights, the colors, and the sounds. I immersed myself in an imaginary experience that was as real as possible, and every day, even if only for a few minutes, I imagined myself triumphant in that space.

Over time, those same images that were only real in my imagination began to manifest in my life, and when that happened, a part of me seemed to know exactly what to do and how to feel. It was as if I had already lived those moments and knew how to handle myself easily and confidently. The brain has no distinction between the imaginary and the real. Indeed, in both cases, a series of physical reactions are triggered. If you don't believe me, imagine yourself chewing on a big piece of a sour lemon. What happens to your body? Do you notice it? This proves that we must be careful with the images we allow in our minds because their consequences are real.

Give it a try! Go ahead with the act of healthy rebellion and see yourself triumphant in situations where you are blocked. The ideal time to conduct this type of visualization exercise is not only before stepping into a certain meeting or when facing a difficult situation. Visualize your triumph in the morning when you wake up or at night before falling asleep. In those two moments, the conscious mind and your ruthless inner judge are less active, so you can proceed to visualize something big for you while experiencing less resistance, self-doubt, and self-judgment.

Choose the feelings that accompany those images

It's of little help to visualize situations of triumph if you feel swallowed by trepidation or deep fears while you do so: you are most likely programming yourself to experience those limiting feelings when you face those situations in real life. It would be best if you allowed yourself to feel an elevated and expansive emotion when you're in the process of winning in your imagination. Give it a try! For example, feeling gratitude towards what you're imagining signals to a part of you that the act has already occurred and went very well, even if it hasn't manifested in your life and the outer does not reflect it yet.

Sometimes, it's not easy to stop feeling fear when pursuing an ambitious goal. What has worked for me to reconnect with the emotions of triumph and gratitude is to remember an important past event in which I felt that way. I travel back to my past, remember those feelings, feel them again, and bring them to the present to merge them with the new visualization I'm working with.

A few decades ago, when I lived in Argentina, I made a meaningful career change. I went from finance and auditing to marketing and brand management by joining a prestigious global company that more than one of my college classmates would have given anything to join. The interview process was not easy: I had to sit for multiple tests similar to those I later took to apply to my master's program at the Tuck School of Business at Dartmouth. I still remember receiving the phone call announcing that the position was mine. The triumph and deep gratitude I felt at that moment were indescribable, and I still remember it as if it were yesterday. Today, when visualizing a big goal, especially one that intimidates me, I concentrate on reviving my emotions when that multinational company invited me to join their ranks.

What would be that moment of achievement and significant expansion for you? For one of my coaching clients, it was receiving her first paycheck and holding it in her hands; for another, becoming a mother after years of treatments and the moment she could hold her baby for the first time. Only you know which event in your life generates a feeling of achievement and deep gratitude; you must identify it now and remember it for the journey we will undertake in the following chapters.

Transform your inner dialogue

In a place where no one else is listening but yourself, how do you speak to yourself, what words do you choose to say to yourself in challenging situations?

A few weeks ago, I went out for dinner with a Latina woman who holds a leadership position at a consumer goods company. As she told me, she had realized that her internal dialogue was blocking her. When she was in meetings with other executives, those inner voices were so strong that they distracted her. She missed part of the conversation, and opportunities to make valuable comments slipped through her fingers.

She is not alone. In my keynotes, I usually conduct anonymous surveys asking participants to identify what their inner critic tells them most often. From *You are not smart enough (or strong, young, or well-connected enough)*, to *Others can do it better than you, Who do you think you are?, You don't deserve to be here!, They will realize you don't know anything* or even *You are a parasite and don't deserve to succeed*. I've heard it all. If, for just one moment, we expressed out loud what goes on inside our heads, more than one person would be horrified. We must stop that internal dialogue and replace it with one supporting us. For example, *I am enough, I deserve to succeed, I am resourceful and can solve what life throws at me, I am valuable, I belong in this place, What I have to say adds value, My experience is meaningful, and it counts.*

What is your loudest voice of self-limitation? Dare to identify it. Then, create a short phrase that stands for the opposite of what that limiting voice screams at you whenever you find yourself in a challenging situation. Now, remember that what you resist persists. So, you change a limiting voice not by beating it up and forcefully silencing it. That is what resistance is about: suppressing, denying, or pushing aside what bothers or shames us. Loving them is how we reduce the volume of those limiting voices. Love your limiting voice, your voices of judgment, and your humanity, along with your strengths and areas of opportunity. Love every part of you with passion, and you will experience the frequency of love, starting to lower the volume of that cruel voice you use to punish and judge yourself. Replacing these voices requires focus, repetition, and discipline, but it is possible. We must be committed if we want to win in our imagination and our inner space.

A few years ago, as an act of healthy rebellion, I decided to place sticky notes all around my house to help me in the process of turning up the volume of my inner voices of self-empowerment. I chose the phrase «I am enough» to begin replacing that «You're Not Good Enough» voice that in 2016 had driven me to overwork myself until I collapsed, and placed the little notes in my workspace, on my bathroom mirror, in my breakfast cereal cupboard, next to my favorite cup of coffee. The power of this simple act has been profoundly transformative. Give it a try!

It is a waste of time to try to change others. It is more efficient and revolutionary to focus on creating our inner reality and forming a new belief system that will allow us to show up in the world with such deep self-confidence that doors will begin to open. People love to join those who vibrate success. Exude success and confidence from every pore of your being, and people will surround you, offering support and resources to create something even greater together.

As seeds bear better fruit when planted in fertile soil, if you want your acts of rebellion and visualization exercises to flourish with deep roots, you must prepare your soil for it to happen. That will create the conditions for growth beyond your wildest dreams. What you need for your fertile soil is not easy to find in this world of frenzy, productivity, and constant stimuli, but it is profoundly healing and transformative. What you need to make your soil fertile is silence.

SILENCE CHANGED MY LIFE

By now, you know that 2016 was one of my toughest years. I was physically, mentally, and emotionally depleted. Those who had seen my rise in elite spaces were unaware of my most intimate reality. I had manifested and achieved, but my doubts and judgments against myself had not ceased. The unsustainable pressure took a toll on my physical and mental health, on my happiness, and even on my desire to live. Many observed me navigating my spaces like a fish in water, not knowing that inside, I was drowning in a sea of doubts, plunged into the clutches of the unattainable pressure to be perfect, and trapped in a desperate search for external approval to fill the deep emptiness I felt. I had flown high, and from that height, my fall was devastating.

—Quit right now and take a few months to think about what you want to do —my husband suggested, his eyes reflecting a deep concern. Never before had he experienced this torn and defeated version of the brave woman he had married 16 years earlier. For many years, I had skillfully hidden my fears, my feelings of inferiority, and my addiction to self-criticism until my collapse exposed this unknown version of a fragile being bent over by her internal struggles.

That day began the deepest transformation I could have ever imagined. In the beginning, everything was challenging. When I quit my job, I felt guilty for not being productive. To calm my mind down, I joined a gym and poured all that energy of commitment and achievement into reaching an enviable physical shape in just a few months. Just as my obsession had been perfectionism and surpassing the expectations of all my superiors in the workplace, I pushed myself at the gym to burn the most calories per hour and be the last standing in the most intense cardio classes. At the same time, my mind demanded: «Keep going, let's do more.» Obviously, I continued with the same patterns of self-punishment and self-torture, but this time, I changed the office and the sound of fingers typing on keyboards for the gym and the blasting music.

It was clear that this would not take me very far. A few months later, in a group classroom packed with people, I got distracted looking at my phone and did not see the 15-pound weight coming towards the left side of my head as my gym neighbor threw her arms out in shoulder blade exercises. It caused me a concussion.

—You need two to three weeks of mental rest at home, without screens and any stimulation from people around you —my doctor prescribed.

A week later, I went back to see her, this time with a fractured foot. I had forgotten my water bottle in the freezer, and when I bent down to grab it, I lost my balance as a consequence of my concussion and dropped the frozen bottle on my bare foot with such bad luck that I broke one of the most fragile and painful bones in my foot. I took that as a clear message from God, telling me something like, «Valeria, as you insist on your self-destructive habits, you will now stay locked in the darkness of your room, immobilized on your bed with a cast on your foot, without the interferences of this world. Maybe now you can go to the only place where your healing can occur: your inner space.» And so it was. I finally understood the message; I had no other choice.

The following two weeks were a combination of darkness to alleviate my migraines, silence to avoid overstimulating my brain, and constant prayers asking for clarity and understanding of why I had gotten myself into that situation. Here and there, I began to remember my childhood and had glimpses of how happy I was with a very simple life. I remembered how much I loved playing with my cousins and siblings in my hometown's unpaved streets during the hot summers when others were taking their siestas — a time when all this about being productive and pushing myself beyond exhaustion did not exist.

The inner silence was not immediate. At first, everything was loud inside, with too many voices of judgment and a constant tsunami of thoughts. As the days went by, the internal noise began to diminish, and I began to experience my inner silence, an unknown, peaceful sensation, and an infinite expansion of my being as if my essence were not reduced to the limits of my physical body. Slowly, and as my «house arrest» came to an end, I found myself allocating time to things I had not allowed myself to enjoy before, such as taking a salt bath, listening to soft music, reading books on spirituality, and even going to therapy for the first time in my life. Perhaps that was not just for crazy people («eso es para locos»), as I had been told.

In the silence, I reconnected with myself and began to love who I am, step by step. I really needed to spend time with myself and give myself space for reconnection. I started to listen within, to take care of and to appreciate myself. When silence became part of my life, I deepened my connection with the energies of peace and gratitude and became more aware of the thoughts going through my head. Silence allowed me to confront my inner life face to face, and although it was not that comfortable, I would do it again one thousand times over, as that reconnection with my being transformed me from the deepest level.

Some time ago, I listened to an interview with the writer Pablo d'Ors titled «Meditation is a radical path to self-knowledge,» he shared revealing ideas about the power of silence, reflection, and meditation to transform our lives. «I do not know a more radical path; I would even dare to say wilder or more direct to self-discovery than the practice of meditation. Or, if you prefer, the practice of inner silencing,» he said. «We live stunned by so many messages, words, sounds, and images,» he expressed, to which he added that «meditation is a practice of silencing that consists of sitting, if possible every day, with your back straight and simply becoming aware of your own body, following the rhythm of your breath.»

> **ACT OF HEALTHY REBELLION**
>
> **Sit in silence for at least 10 minutes.**
>
> Become aware of your inner world and awaken your love for your highest version. What this unconditional love brings into your life may become the greatest act of healthy rebellion you can allow yourself to experience. Let your inner silence give birth to a roar that will propel you toward the most powerful version of yourself.

D'Ors explained how difficult it can be to stay still because that will cause us to notice the inner chatter we constantly experience. This chatter can be so overwhelming that most of us cannot tolerate it and cut off meditation to do «something more productive.» However, if we persevere in achieving this progressive inner silence, we will see its fruits in the long run. According to D'Ors, the first fruits are clarity and courage to act. I can attest that this has been the case with me. In the silence, I gained clarity on my life purpose, and in that space, I also found the courage to stand up and speak up in front of hundreds, when only a few years before, I would sweat profusely and feel terrified if I had to speak up in front of two people.

Don't wait for life to bring you to your knees to give yourself the gift of silence and the opportunity to discover who you are. Do you want to rebel against a system where you feel minimized, invisible, and undervalued? Sit with yourself in silence.

> **LESSONS LEARNED**
>
> - The formula for creating change that the world taught us (Results → Behaviors → Internal Reality) is entirely backward. If, instead of trying to change our results, we start by changing our internal reality, we will exhibit a series of adjusted behaviors that will, in turn, manifest different results.
> - Your inner transformation depends on three fundamental and simultaneous components: the images of yourself that you hold in your mind, the feelings that go hand in hand with those images, and your inner dialogue.
> - Win in your imagination. When it comes to the images in your mind, focus on positive and triumphant images, not catastrophic ones that only unbalance you and create stress.
> - Accompany those triumphant images with expansive feelings: replace fear or other limiting feelings with gratitude, as this signals your brain that the event has already occurred and everything went very well.
> - Become aware of your inner dialogue and pivot it. How do you talk to yourself? What words do you choose to say to yourself in challenging situations? Identify your most limiting voice and replace it with the opposite phrase.
> - Create spaces of silence in your day-to-day life, as this is where your deepest transformation will flourish. At first, it may seem that your inner noise is amplified, but with perseverance and patience, you will begin to connect with your deepest essence and have more clarity on your life purpose.

CHAPTER 7

Can you succeed by being yourself?

How many times have we heard phrases like «Be yourself,» «Be authentic,» and «Be proud of your roots and your values and show them to the world without fear»? We have also been told that diversity, which includes us, is good for business and adds value to society. Several studies by the consulting firm McKinsey indicate that companies with greater ethnic and racial diversity among their executives generate higher profits. Still, we wonder whether it will be good for us to show up authentically as we are. Every time I hear those kinds of phrases, my inner voices and alarms go off as, more than once, being authentic backfired quite severely for me: *If I show myself as I am, doors may close; If I express myself in the way that comes most naturally to me, they will say that I move my hands too much or raise my voice too much, or even judge me as aggressive or too emotional; If I show myself firm and self-confident, they will say that I am confrontational and that may harm my reputation; If I say exactly what I think, clients will stop working with me; There is a good opportunity on the horizon and showing myself as «very Latina» at this moment can play against me.*

Men are not subjected to the same kind of pressure. They are seen as good leaders when they show up and speak confidently. They are considered excellent dads when they request time to take their children to the doctor or attend their school play. At the same time, we, the eternal tightrope walkers, have to change who we are, our interests, and how we tend to express ourselves most naturally to please a world that has already passed judgment on our value and ability to do our work with excellence, even before we opened our mouth. Let's go back a bit to understand how we got here.

The day you came into the world, you did so as pure potential. Let's use the analogy of a book with hundreds of blank pages from where the purest and brightest light radiates, promising hope and change for humanity. Those pages would begin to be written from each experience, each encounter, each word that reached your ears, and each situation your eyes witnessed. It is possible that during your first years of life, you wrote in your book with complete freedom and confidence, and without fear, filling those pages with your essence and your true self. It is also possible that as you grew up, you held your book and raised it high for the world to see as you were beaming with pride, and you received responses such as *Not like that*, *You're doing it wrong*, or *People like you don't achieve those kinds of dreams*. It is possible that, with your heart a bit broken, you began to cross out some of the pages you had written, that you tore out some others to throw them away, or that you grabbed other papers and pasted them on top of your original expression, shamefully covering what for you had been your pure essence but for the world was not perfect or insufficient.

When I was eight, I started taking English classes in my hometown. My parents gave me two options back then: piano or studying languages. I answered, «Both!» but the family budget only allowed one of those alternatives. I still remember the enthusiasm I had every time I rode my bike to the small house of white walls near the downtown area where classes took place. One particular day stands out among many memories. While we waited for the class to start, my classmates and I sat around a rectangular table near a large window through which the afternoon sun was streaming in. My enthusiasm for learning a new language was almost as great as the joy of making new friends, so you can imagine how happy I was with friends sitting around the table. Beyond excited and perhaps talking a bit too loudly, I would tell them about a new game my cousins and I came up with or about my plans for after class that afternoon.

—Be silent for a change, Valeria! —the slamming door startled me so much that I felt like someone had poured a bucket of ice water on me. The English teacher, a young woman in her 20s, walked towards me while keeping her eyes fixed on me. She didn't look very happy. It seemed she had wanted to start her class, and I, totally immersed in my experience, hadn't even realized that she had entered the room until she slammed the door shut, like a judge loudly banging the gavel to call the room to order. —How many times do I have to tell you to shut your mouth?! —she fired off like an invisible slap that hit me full force. My 8-year-old humanity didn't know where to hide. I felt the heat of shame rising on my neck and face. I immediately felt like crying, but I held it back. Still staring me in the eyes, she let all her frustration out:— You were so shy on the first day of class, and now I can't get you to shut up! I will have to talk to your mother if you continue like this.

That day marked me deeply. From then on, I decided that the part of me that was fun, that spoke with total authenticity, and that laughed every three sentences could put me in danger and subject me to humiliation and shame. It is better to stay quiet to avoid negative consequences. That's what I did for many years, including the remaining time at elementary school, high school, college, my multiple jobs, and, until very recently, as the owner of my business.

Events from the past that seem irrelevant or small may have profoundly wounded us, pushing us to make decisions that have consequences for years or even decades. This was my case when I decided that silence would be my safe space and that my authentic expression should be hidden because it could bring me humiliation, shame, and rejection from authority figures.

Rejection can mark us deeply, especially when we are growing up. It can plague us with self-doubt, convincing us to hide our talents, conceal our value, and rob us of the opportunity to offer our greatness to the world. In my case, external rejection gave rise to self-rejection because, from that day on, I disassociated from that part of me that was free and authentic. I chained her feet and hands and put a very thick piece of adhesive tape on the mouth of that 8-year-old girl. I limited her free expression.

> **ACT OF HEALTHY REBELLION**
>
> **Remember events that marked your life,
> like the one above marked mine, and reflect:**
>
> *What decisions did I make then regarding myself,
> authority figures, and the world in general?*
>
> _____
>
> _____
>
> _____
>
> _____
>
> We will work on this again later.

When I revisited my past to heal those events that had wounded me, I discovered that my powerful essence and innate potential were still there. No matter how many layers I had placed on top to protect myself or how much of my essence I had tried to toss away like a paper ball, the reality of who we are eventually clamors to come out in freedom. It's now time. The light destined to shine brightly cannot be hidden for too long: sooner or later, it begins to seep through the small cracks, eventually urges for its freedom, and seeks to shine in all its magnitude. Now, I learned from other women with similar experiences as mine that if you let that light out in all its splendor, you will most likely blind those who are not used to the type of glow that you emit. So, can you succeed by being yourself? Or are you condemned to show a version of yourself that has been edited a thousand times and doesn't feel entirely authentic?

To support you on the path of discovering what is best for you at each moment, we will embark on a journey of identifying and removing some of those protective layers you have placed to cover your greatness, and in the next chapter, we will explore different ways in which you can show up to the world while honoring your essence.

With all these questions, I got together with Silvana Montenegro, an executive at a renowned global financial services firm. Silvana and I crossed paths some time ago when Lupita Colmenero, chief operating officer at Latina Style and a dear mutual friend, introduced us. I immediately noticed something unique about Silvana. Unlike other Latina leaders who reached positions of power, she did not change who she was and kept showing up with an energy of authenticity. I knew when we met that if I had continued my corporate career, that is precisely how I would have liked to show up as a leader. But coming from that space, I also knew how difficult it can be to succeed in being yourself, especially when you are one of the few Latina women in executive spaces. My admiration and respect for Silvana were immediate, and I knew that I had to follow up with her privately to understand how she had managed to keep her essence intact in one of the most competitive and demanding spaces.

That Fall afternoon in New York, I had the opportunity to have a fascinating conversation with this successful immigrant woman, wife, daughter, and mother of two. Her openness and authenticity only increased my appreciation for her. Silvana is an example of the new leadership, and she wears it on her sleeve.

—How do you do it, Silvana? —I asked her very directly—. I want to understand how you present yourself by being you, by being authentic. How has your experience been?

—It's still a constant effort —she confessed with the authenticity that characterizes her.

When Silvana lived in Brazil, she didn't need to overthink her identity. She was Brazilian, period. She didn't hesitate to express her ideas in meetings, and displaying self-confidence, she led complex projects that impacted her country and the entire Latin American region. When she arrived in the United States more than twenty years ago, pursuing a once-in-a-lifetime growth opportunity within her organization, she encountered a reality that confused her and led her to doubt herself and the talents with which she had built her professional success up to that point. I am sure many of us can relate to that story.

—Suddenly, I was assigned the label «Hispanic» without me understanding what that really meant — she told me. —With this new identity that was not so clear to me, I went from a culture where it was okay to talk about how your weekend went and where hugs were a common form of greeting to a culture where conversations went straight to business topics, efficiently and directly to the point.

Silvana's cultural adjustment was uncomfortable because she could not find other women like her in those meeting rooms. She was primarily surrounded by men, none of whom were Latino. Sometimes, she felt like a newcomer and different from the assertive and confident leader she had been just a few weeks ago in her homeland.

Her feeling of insecurity was immediate and profoundly immobilizing. Silvana opted to remain in a safe space, observing a lot and speaking little until she understood a bit more about her new environment.

—For a long time I suffered in silence —this woman, who had left her family and boyfriend behind in her homeland, shared—. I questioned everything about myself, and to a certain extent, I nullified my authentic self to try to assimilate.

Silvana ended up completely exhausted every single day. The enormous cultural change and all those unknown emotions were too much for her head and heart.

THE POWER OF OUR ALLIES
TO HELP US UNBLOCK

At some point, our lives cross paths with people, or with angels indeed, who genuinely care about our well-being and success and who know to appreciate what makes us unique. That is what happened to Silvana.

—Silvana, your style is very different but very effective —one of the organization's leaders who had been watching her closely told her. Those nine words triggered a radical shift in how Silvana saw herself and became the push she needed to show more of herself, contribute her ideas, and build relationships with others as only she knew how. That leader, an ally, had noticed that Silvana went to meetings with a clear agenda and a vision to mobilize the team in that direction. Those strengths set her apart from others and did not go unnoticed.

—That's how, little by little, I came out of the closet as myself —Silvana told me—. At first, I shared my ideas with a bit of fear, but I intended to continue pushing myself out of my comfort zone. I took small steps and closely observed how those around me reacted. To my surprise, my performance evaluations were very positive. I took all that information as a sign that I was on the right track.

The surprise Silvana expresses seems familiar. In my early years in the United States, I expected that my performance evaluations would be horrible or that I would soon be fired.

Instead, I found myself with salary increases and promotions. Cultural and communication differences lead us to lose sight of how valuable our work is. That's why it's so important to request feedback more often. We are encouraged to bring more of our true essence when we know we are on the right track.

According to a Harvard Business Review study, 76% of Latinos in the United States feel that we cannot bring our whole selves to work. That same study indicates that 43% of Latina women and 33% of Latino men express that they must limit their expression to align with their company's standards and expectations.

How many of us have been told not to be so emotional, to use a more «Anglo» name, or, at a minimum, to modify the pronunciation of our name to make it easier for English speakers? Thus, little by little, we assimilate our style to the male, white standards that represent the model of professional success in the collective unconscious.

Trying to create change by sheer force can carry a high cost, particularly when we push from a place of survival. When microaggressions and discrimination are present in the workplace, you may feel that you have no choice but to suppress those parts of you that would draw too much attention or that would make others consider you too emotional, problematic, or aggressive. The problem is that this forced suppression out of fear has real consequences on your physical, mental, and emotional health.

An article by CALDA Clinic that analyzed the physical and mental health consequences for those who suppress their emotions to be accepted by their environment concluded that this effort increases the sympathetic nervous system activity, with an immediate impact on cardiovascular activity, increased blood pressure, heart problems, and other long-term diseases. In other words, a forced suppression of personality carries a high cost that is not only emotional but also physical, and it can turn into a silent illness. Our bodies take a toll.

Even though the many powerful lessons shaped Silvana's path twenty years ago, she carries them with her to this day.

—We can only reach our potential if we accept who we truly are —she asserts—. What makes us unique is a gift that we bring to our spaces, and we cannot afford to keep it hidden.

EXPRESS YOURSELF WITH AUTHENTICITY

On the journey to becoming my authentic self at work, I sought a roadmap to help me identify my value and make it visible to others. Interestingly, I found that map amidst what I had learned in the marketing industry. Around 1999, when I was working at Procter & Gamble, my team was challenged to reposition the brand Pantene. While Pantene was perceived in other countries as a premium brand for women who wanted silky and soft hair, in Argentina, it had the collective perception of being a product for men's hair loss. Nothing further apart from each other as the image of a woman with long, shiny hair and that of a bold man!

The process of helping consumers understand the actual value of this brand required several steps. It began with identifying the exact product attributes. What made Pantene a brand that was effective and superior for female hair? Then, we studied the psychology of our female audience to figure out how we could influence them to trust the brand. This was a complex strategic marketing case because we had to change the way the product was perceived in people's minds. As Latinas, we face a similar challenge. We first have to know ourselves in depth, understand what we bring to the table that is unique and different, and then get to know our audience to influence them to trust us.

Step 1: Know yourself and define your brand

This first step is critical. We added so many layers to protect ourselves that we have disconnected from our essence. This first step involves deeply reconnecting with who you are, not with who someone told you to be. This transcends your current position or role. Your brand is who you are and goes beyond the position you occupy today or the business you oversee. Create a brand aligned with your identity that you can take wherever you go.

So many times, we resist seeing who we are. As America Ferrera says in her TED Talk *My identity is a superpower, not an obstacle*: «I couldn't change what a system believed about me, while I believed what the system believed about me. I am just one of the millions of people who have been told that in order to fulfill my dreams, in order to contribute my talents to the world, I have to resist the truth of who I am. I for one, am ready to stop resisting and to start existing as my full and authentic self.»

ACT OF HEALTHY REBELLION

Embark with an open heart on the process of rediscovery and answer the following questions:

Who am I? What adjectives describe me? Examples: resilient, committed, creative, brave...

_____

_____

_____

What experiences make my brand unique and different? Perhaps you have paved your way through multiple cultures, spoken several languages, or worked in different industries. Your titles and certifications also matter, as do your life experiences. For example, if you were a translator for your immigrant parents as a child, then you were pushed to be a leader from a young age and may have developed the ability to navigate through different spaces and cultures. All of that has great value.

_____

_____

_____

What values are important to me?
It could be dedication to work, honest communication, loyalty, commitment to self-improvement, or the ability to create solid interpersonal relationships.

_____

_____

_____

Identify which of those values are present in the people around you, as this can help you find allies and mentors. Also, identify which of those values is recognized by your organization, as it is in your best interest to make them more visible.

_____

_____

_____

I leave you with a final thought: every brand that earns the trust of its consumers has to deliver what it promises to do. If Pantene pledges to leave your hair soft and shiny and instead leaves it dull and entangled, would you keep buying it? Probably not. So, ensure you do the expected job excellently to earn others' trust and create long-term loyalty toward you.

Step 2: Clarify your definition of success

Each person has their definition of success. Dare to look into what makes you happy, setting aside what the world wants you to think and choose. In the early stages of my career, I defined my success by my annual salary and title. When I launched my business, I measured my success by the number of clients and annual revenue. Over time, I realized these were short-term goals: essential milestones but insufficient to encompass the transcendental meaning I seek through my work. Talking to Silvana, I discovered she had reached a similar conclusion.

—There came a point when I said: «If this is it for my career, good. If I go further, that's fine too.» I never had the ambition to reach the top just for the sake of reaching it, only to achieve personal goals that demanded that I leave aside my health, family, and happiness —Silvana said—. My ambition is to have an impact on the lives of others, have the platform to empower and support them, and be respected for who I am and what I contribute. Of course, title and salary are necessary but not sufficient.

As mothers, we both understand that being successful means keeping ourselves healthy, happy, and present so our children can be too. If we suffer a setback, we can drag several people down with us; therefore, putting ourselves first and taking care of ourselves physically, mentally, and emotionally is crucial to our success and that of the people we love.

In the short term, Silvana has her goals for promotion and salary increases, just as I have my own in my consulting work and as a keynote speaker. However, we also have goals related to our health, rest, physical exercise, and the amount of quality time we want to spend with our children and other loved ones.

My definition of success in its transcendental sense has two components: *impact* and *personal fulfillment*. What is your personal and transcendental definition of success? What are your short-term goals? Take detailed notes and ensure they are truly yours and not those of your parents, partner, the rest of the family, or society. If you seem not to be reaching your goals at any given moment, consider replacing the word *failure* with *learning*. For me, being successful means constantly adjusting what needs to be adjusted, looking at each obstacle as a learning experience for my continuous growth.

Step 3: Understand your audience

Most people go through the world trying to convince others, sell them something, or gain their approval without first placing themselves in those people's shoes and understanding their interests. For Pantene, this would have been the equivalent of wasting millions of dollars on marketing campaigns, insisting that women buy a product they perceived was made for bold men. We first need to understand what motivates them to buy haircare products and what changes we should make in the packaging or brand positioning to change the brand's perception. Unless we do this, results can be minimal and unsustainable in the long run, no matter how hard we push and deplete ourselves.

Something similar happens with your professional brand. If you want to do it differently from the majority around you, take the time to understand your audience in detail. This requires discipline, concentration, and flexibility since each circumstance will differ depending on who is in the room. Ask yourself:

- What motivates each of these people? How can I encourage them to have them on my side?
- What values, interests, and activities (inside and outside the professional space) do I have in common with this person?
- What type of ideas or projects does this person tend to approve? Why?
- How would each person in the room react to my proposed idea? What objections may arise based on each person's objectives?
- What part of this idea would benefit those in the room, and what part will generate complications or additional work for them?
- How can we resolve those complications in a way that we all win?

These are just some possible initial questions. What's important here is that you take the time to place yourself in others' shoes and create the experience of moving them toward your vision in your mind. Learn to read people and to anticipate what each person will say and how they will react. Learn to observe the dynamics, personal interests, and power plays, assuming the role of a neutral observer so that these dynamics don't exhaust you. As Silvana did, observe, listen, and evaluate the environment to facilitate your success in those spaces.

Step 4: Let go of the need for external validation

As you express your authenticity, you may find that the environment doesn't always welcome you with open arms. At that moment, you will need to decide whether you accept yourself as you are or if you will allow the exhausting back-and-forth of seeking others' approval.

Mónica Márquez is a co-founder of the successful venture Beyond Barriers, which helps leading companies accelerate their growth by supporting the development of their diverse talent. Mónica proudly belongs to the reduced group of Latina entrepreneurs who raised more than two million dollars from investors. Some time ago, I learned about her journey to express her authentic self as a member of the LGBTQIA+ community (if there's one group in our culture that faces rejection from our own, it's the LGBTQIA+ community).

—One of the most difficult processes of my life was coming out as a gay Latina —she said—. For years, I tried to comply with the norms society had imposed on me and the pressure to be the perfect Latina daughter. For a long time, I suffered from my internal struggles since I had a belief that if I came out, those around me would reject me.

Over time, Mónica noticed how much of her happiness and self-appreciation depended on external validation. She felt the pressure to be accepted, to belong, and, in her own words, to «be normal.»

Every human being has the fundamental need to be loved and valued. Those of us who at some point believed that who we were is not okay, or those who have been wounded in our self-esteem or pride when we showed up authentically as who we were, may have believed that who we are doesn't deserve to be loved. This creates an inner void we desperately try to fill with external things, particularly with others' approval. We do it to feel once again that who we are is okay. And in general, that does not end well.

—I felt miserable living with what felt was a facade, a mask that didn't allow me to be my authentic self —Mónica continued—. I overcompensated and worked very hard to be perfect in all other aspects so that when they discovered who I was, they wouldn't reject me as much as there would be other things to balance it out. It was horrible. I fell into extreme exhaustion, and there came a point when I became very sick.

At 29, Mónica moved from her small town in West Texas to New York City. She wanted to distance herself from her loved ones to connect with her authentic essence. Through inner work and therapy, she realized that the only way she would be happy was to let go of the need for all this external validation. When she decided to accept herself fully, things changed dramatically.

—When you normalize what makes you who you are regardless of what others say, you experience a great liberation. It's like unlocking a power you didn't realize you had because your energy was constantly used to cover up a part of you.

A study by Sylvia Ann Hewlet indicates that «coming out of the closet» definitely makes a difference in our professional lives. In middle management, the number of LGBTQIA+ professionals in or out of the closet is very similar (49% out, 51% in). But if you look at senior executives, you find that the majority of LGBTQIA+ professionals in those positions have already come out of the closet (71% versus 29% who have not yet done so). In other words, career progression can accelerate when our energy is focused on projects and results, not on editing ourselves.

As Latinas, we are called to be especially intentional about freeing ourselves from seeking the approval of others. Let's leave behind the «what will people say» (*qué va a decir la gente*) to unleash our maximum potential. After all, it's good for us, and it's good for business.

Any profound change starts with making new decisions that will replace the outdated ones we made in the past. In the same way that as a child, I had decided to call myself to invisibility and silence for fear of being hurt, decades later, I decided to be authentic and express my true voice, even when it makes me uncomfortable or when I feel a little afraid. Just as Silvana had decided that she should initially observe a lot and speak little to find her place, she decided to own her space and lead with the unique qualities she brought. Mónica had shrunk her expression and essence for fear of rejection, and then she decided to give herself the approval she had been seeking in the world.

The world needs more Silvanas and Mónicas because as they gave themselves the freedom to be who they are, they signaled to others that it was OK to provide themselves with the freedom to show up as their authentic selves. When you decide that there is nothing wrong with you and make the decision to love yourself in your totality, authenticity will flow through your pores in a way that is impossible to contain. Love for yourself is an energetic vibration that reaches out to those around you. It shows you are full of confidence and somebody with something important to say that others will want to listen and respect. Right here, we can find your great act of healthy rebellion: give yourself the approval and love you have been waiting to receive from the outside, and that will be the portal to show the world who you really are.

ACT OF HEALTHY REBELLION

Go back to the list of decisions you made at the beginning of the chapter and reflect:

Which of these decisions can I change?

_____

_____

_____

_____

_____

Your success, health, and happiness will depend on these new decisions.

LESSONS LEARNED

- We came into the world as pure potential, but experiences, labels, and others' judgments made us slowly cover up what was our essence because it wasn't perfect or enough for the world.

- 76% of Latinos and Latinas suppress parts of our persona at work, modifying our appearance, body language, and communication style. This suppression has real consequences on our emotional and physical health.

- No matter how many layers of protection we have put on who we really are, we clamor to emerge because the light meant to shine brightly cannot be hidden. Our allies can be vital in letting that light shine.

- To showcase the value of our professional brand, we can use what we observe in trusted brands as a guide. First, it's important to know who we are, understand what we bring to the table, and get to know our audience to influence them to open their hearts and minds to accept and trust us.

- We can only reach our potential if we accept ourselves as we truly are because what makes us unique is a great gift that we bring to our spaces. As we give ourselves the freedom to be who we are, we will change the system by giving others that same freedom to show up as themselves.

CHAPTER 8

Break the silence and talk about yourself

Millions of Latina women have been taught to remain silent, especially in ambiguous, conflicting, or uncomfortable situations. Cultural beliefs also discourage us from talking about ourselves, equating it with being too selfish, leading many of us to be excessively modest or humble. This mindset can be problematic in the United States, where staying silent or making oneself invisible can result in missed opportunities and disadvantages.

Breaking our silence is not just about using our words for self-expression but also about intentionally making ourselves visible to be seen as active and involved. Think of a brand you love because it does the work it promises and does it very well. What good is it to keep it hidden and deprive the world of its benefits? Something similar happens with us. Every time specific cultural messages influence our actions, such as *Work hard and someone will notice someday, You look prettier when you're silent (Calladita te ves mas bonita)*, or *Don't give your opinion if it gets you in trouble*, we are not the only ones who lose: the world around us also loses.

Nature is wise. Have you observed that nature takes up mostly all empty spaces? I remember a photo my friend Mónica showed me some time ago. That picture showed several feet of blacktop with a narrow crack at the center. A beautiful red flower had grown out of that crack, which seemed almost impossible. Nature rarely leaves empty spaces; it fills them with something. Similarly, if you stay silent when you are expected to contribute, don't think there won't be consequences. Just as nature grows in the most unusual crevices, people around you will fill in the gaps and conclude things about you, even if you haven't said a word, especially if you haven't said a word.

With your silence, you can create in others all kinds of perceptions that do not benefit you, such as that you may not be motivated with your work, that you may be unfamiliar with the subject, or that you may not be leadership material, all because in some key moments others do not see what you are capable of contributing. I am not trying to pressure you to speak or become visible without being prepared, but rather to shed light on the actual consequences that our community faces due to that ancestral cultural belief that women should put their heads down, work hard, and prioritize serving others, instead of going out visibly into the world as change agents. Let's admit that history gave us a secondary role in which our voice was not heard much. Today, using our voice is critical to becoming a force of change for this country and the world.

How many times have we heard that we need to be less modest and show more of who we are? However, we are not being told exactly how to do that. Without that roadmap, we may speak up while being visibly uncomfortable, perhaps generating the opposite effect of what we wanted to achieve. In the following pages, you will learn how to act with confidence and a variety of techniques for using your voice that you can implement depending on the situation you find yourself in.

BECOME YOUR NUMBER ONE FAN

If you are committed to a process of profound personal transformation, there is a necessary step that you cannot skip: developing unconditional love for yourself. Love forgives everything, and we need to forgive ourselves for the many times we made mistakes; love hopes for everything, and we need to dare to dream big; love believes in everything, and we need to believe in ourselves like never before.

To the willingness to love yourself, add daily and intentional moments to accept yourself as you are, even when those around you may not entirely accept you. Decide to be the one who loves every part of you, including your voices of judgment and insecurity and your stumbles on your learning path. Become your most loyal fan who forgives your mistakes, gives you new opportunities, and believes in you after things don't go as planned. Loving yourself is a decision. You can make it at this moment and renew it every day. Acting like your number one fan, agent, and representative will give you the strength and courage to go out into the world with pride to show who you are, ask for what you deserve, and stand up for your interests without fear.

I know this because I experienced it. The day I decided to love who I am as I am instead of criticizing myself, a decision I need to renew frequently, many things started to change, including how I talk about myself to others, how I advocate for myself without shame, and how I set boundaries with dignity. Love and respect for yourself are the key pillars for everything that follows and are necessary daily decisions.

DARE TO SHOW MORE OF YOURSELF

Because many perceive us as humble and modest, this has become a stereotype about who we are and an expectation of how we should generally behave. Taking action to break the silence and our stereotypical image of excessive modesty does not only involve talking about your achievements in the workplace; it's also about communicating more about who you are, your interests outside of work, your volunteer activities, and everything that makes you proudly you.

The art of talking about oneself with naturality is precisely that: an art that is learned and developed through observation and practice. Be prepared to make your brushstrokes when the opportunity to talk about yourself arises. Those in my circle know that I take every opportunity to mention my work as an author and speaker, my volunteer activities and contributions to the community, and even specific anecdotes from my family environment. How do I do it so that it sounds natural? I stay absolutely present and immersed in the dialogue taking place. As soon as my mind makes a connection between the topic being discussed and my work and interests, I take the opportunity to share an interesting anecdote or insight that provides value to my interlocutor. Sometimes, I do it for them to get to know me better or to find common ground that will allow me to deepen our relationship, other times, I seek to break the ice so that the other person will share more about themselves.

Be strategic: every interaction is an opportunity to grow your brand. And remember, it's not about the words you say but the energy you radiate and how you make your interlocutor feel.

WHEN FACING CONFLICT, SHOW UP

Those moments when your survival instinct prompts you to hide and save your energy for the next battle are when you have the most incredible opportunity to give visibility and grow your brand. In other words, when our cultural instinct invites us to flee and take refuge in silence, our actions and words can make the greatest impact.

Conflictive situations invite us to act with determination and awareness. I like how Lisa, a vice president at a healthcare company, explains it using the acronym WAIT.

—The acronym WAIT helps me pause for a second to ask myself, «**W**hy **A**m **I T**alking?» —Lisa explained.

> **ACT OF HEALTHY REBELLION**
>
> ***Visualize yourself in a conflictive situation where you remained silent while you had something to contribute. Reflect:***
>
> *What could I have done differently?*
> *What can I apply in future situations?*
>
> _____
>
> _____
>
> _____
>
> _____

Uncomfortable moments of disagreement or conflict allow you to position yourself as a valuable leader. Still, for that to happen, you must be strategic and clear on what you seek when you speak up or intervene. What do you want to achieve from the audience? Where do you want to move them? What part of yourself should you bring at that moment: your negotiating side, the reconciling one, the one that suggests addressing the issue offline, or the one that recommends further investigating the matter before making a final decision?

When Lisa gets «caught in the middle of the battle,» she does not take refuge in silence or invisibility. On the contrary, she takes the opportunity to show what she is capable of.

—A technique that worked very well for me to guide conflictive or ambivalent discussions towards a resolution is to imagine holding a mirror in front of others —Lisa explained—. I am not just giving my opinion, which, of course, is important, but I first reflect on all I researched on the subject and what I have heard from them. I repeat what I heard from the different parties and offer alternative solutions. Making other people feel listened to can work wonders to lower the intensity of discussions.

FOCUS ON RELATIONSHIPS

Lisa's role is to challenge the status quo, which has more than once made her uncomfortable.

—My own insecurities were holding me back to the point that I felt intimidated about raising new ideas in front of other leaders in the organization —she confessed—. I had to change my thinking and become very attuned to the signs of stress in my body during those situations. I learned to work with them.

To overcome her insecurities, Lisa initiated casual conversations with different people within the company, to the point that she developed friendships.

—It's not the same for someone you don't know well to say to you, «This isn't working!» as it is for someone you have a trusting relationship with to say it to you. The words reach you differently, and you no longer wear a protective shell. Everything starts to flow better for everyone.

As an entrepreneur, I can relate to what Lisa is saying. In many cases, my clients' relationships evolved into friendships that I want to treasure for life. At first, I questioned whether it would be good for my business to have those close relationships or if it would be wiser to maintain distance and formality. Over time, I realized that this closeness allowed us to explore better solutions to their problems. I also observed that our cultural warmth is well received and benefits these relationships. Personally, being warm and human has been a great asset. It aligns with my authentic self and is a competitive advantage to help me do a better job.

UNCOMFORTABLE? LET YOUR VALUES GUIDE YOU

In one of my last corporate jobs before my collapse, I had the opportunity to regroup with the company's president to answer one question he had asked me upon learning about my departure: What can we do better?

I had submitted my resignation just a few days before, and this was the first time this leader asked me for feedback. His style up to that point had been to impose his way of thinking and his decisions. So now I had a dilemma since telling him what I really thought could put him on the defensive and close the door for me. On the other hand, masking what I honestly thought by giving a superficial response would harm my professional image. I decided to let my values guide me: courage, integrity, and respectfully speaking truth with a focus on building and not on criticizing. The meeting was excellent. When you speak from your deepest values, you speak from your heart, and your words carry the most powerful energy you can express.

When you doubt how to proceed, return to the values you identified in the previous chapter and let them guide your actions. Your values are deeply connected to your essence and your authentic self. Let them guide you in handling uncomfortable or conflictive situations because connecting with that inner wisdom allows you to show up with confidence and power, and people notice it.

DARE TO BE DIFFERENT

A vital marketing concept called «point of differentiation» refers to what differentiates a brand from its competition. Marketing experts seek to identify this point because they know it is one of the primary keys to the brand's success in the market. Those who identify and communicate their point of differentiation can stand out in a sea of products and services that promise the same result. Isn't it ironic that so many of us feel forced to blend in with everyone else, hiding what makes us unique when that is precisely the shortest path to a product's extinction in the marketing world?

Building your professional brand and expressing yourself authentically is not about having the loudest voice in the room but about contributing what you, and only you, can bring to the conversation: your point of differentiation!

We tend to discount information we acquire through life experiences, thinking others also possess that information. You will be surprised how many times this is not the case.

Adriana Dawson is an executive at a telecommunications company and the daughter of Colombian immigrants. During her childhood, like so many millions of Latino boys and girls, she faced all kinds of difficult and painful situations as a translator for her parents and several members of the community.

—My mom would come home from working at the factory and say to me, «Come on, we have to help my friend fill out some tax papers,» or «Come on, let's go help dad's friend who has a doctor's appointment» —Adriana recalls—. It was traumatic for me to hear how some adults spoke severely about my parents or other members of our community in front of me. It happened to me that the person behind the counter would turn around and say to their coworker in English, «I can't believe these people!» with a derogatory tone while I stood right there, with 12 years old.

Through these experiences, Adriana witnessed the injustices, discrimination, racism, language barriers, and the lack of access to certain key services that so many individuals in our community faced. None of this knowledge and experiences would be in vain as she eventually had the opportunity to dare to be unique and act as a bridge between two cultures.

—It took me some time and a lot of reflection to transition from *I can't believe I lived through this* to *These are life lessons that I can use to guide decisions that impact our community* —Adriana remembers the day she was sitting at a table where most were not Latino—. We were evaluating the launch of a program in a region where most families were Latino, and I noticed the disconnect between the program's objectives and the reality of the families we sought to serve.

Adriana did not hesitate to contribute what only she could add:

—We must provide transportation services since public transportation does not reach the area of the event, and families in that region are multigenerational and do not have vehicles to transport their entire family —she pointed out firmly, knowing precisely what she was talking about having lived it firsthand—, and it is up to us to produce marketing materials in English and Spanish, if we want to reach as many families as possible.

ACT OF HEALTHY REBELLION

Reflect:

What experiences make me unique and valuable in my profession?

_____

_____

_____

_____

Do not refrain from offering your ideas because you think the person next to you will find them obvious. You hold the keys to the cultural knowledge that will allow companies to access the Latino market more successfully, the fastest-growing segment in the United States.

SET BOUNDARIES WITH DIGNITY

Remember Natalia, who had traveled to Germany with a team of engineers and faced her boss's «Shut up! I need to think!" in front of a group of men? Well, that story doesn't end with Natalia's silence.

Natalia had arrived in Miami with her mom at the age of 11. Her mother, the general manager of an insurance company in her home country, had no choice but to clean houses to make ends meet in the United States.

—We were Batman and Robin. Two women against the world, united —Natalia told me—. Observing my mom's strength to get us ahead by herself in a foreign country gave me the strength to stand up for myself and set boundaries with that boss who had silenced me.

Until then, Natalia had found that her co-workers ignored what she asked them to do.

—They didn't take me seriously. Imagine a young Latina giving instructions to middle-aged white men. They wanted nothing to do with me, and after that silencing, it would be even worse. —So, Natalia decided to take matters into her own hands—. Speaking up when facing microaggressions or *machismo* is not just about standing up for yourself —this young woman of profound wisdom told me—. Many times, it consists of explaining to specific leaders what we are capable of and how we like to be treated, particularly when they have no experience managing talent of color or don't know how much we are worth.

When they returned from the day's meetings, Natalia took advantage of a moment alone with her project leader.

—John, you have a Latina daughter like me, right? —she asked her boss while he looked at her with curiosity—. I was thinking that when your daughter grows up, she may face the same difficult situations that I face daily, you know? —And allowing herself to express her truth, she added—: I don't think you would like it if someone treated your daughter the way you treated me today in front of the team —John's face completely changed, and regret was briefly reflected in his eyes. Natalia continued—: When you told me to shut up like that, you took away from me the merit of being the only woman chosen for this international trip.

Her boss apologized, visibly ashamed. But it didn't end there. The next day, as they began their third day of meetings in Germany, John gathered the team and told them:

—I want to apologize to Natalia because how we have treated her is unacceptable. She worked very hard to earn this space and deserves our respect and support to achieve the goals she pursues with her work.

That day, Natalia learned that we can worsen our situation when we don't confront these events for fear of creating more conflict. However, if we can guide others to put themselves in our shoes, we can lay the foundation for a better working relationship, as she did. From that day on, John became her mentor and sponsor, and he wrote her a letter of recommendation for her admission to Yale for her Master's in Business (MBA).

USE CODE-SWITCHING TO YOUR ADVANTAGE

Code-switching consists of changing our behaviors, way of speaking, and even our gestures to adapt to a cultural norm different from the one we were born or raised in. Code-switching is controversial, as many people see it as suppressing their true selves when navigating spaces where they are a minority. I invite you to consider code-switching as the ability to temporarily adapt to the environment, aiming to reach our audience in terms they understand and relate, to achieve our objectives.

We live in a fragmented society where we feel that to be accepted we must change who we are, almost placing our identity on the side. Code-switching has existed for centuries, but most recently, it has been frowned upon and not seen as a valuable tool. What if we reframed code-switching as changing our clothes depending on the occasion without changing who we are? What would happen if we allowed ourselves to experiment with a different outfit without changing our unique essence?

Our Latino community has extensive experience with code-switching. Do we speak to our families in the same way that we speak at work? Do we use the same tone of voice and speech speed with different family members? From a young age, we handled code-switching almost without realizing it. So, why not bring it as a tool to our professional space?

Neuro-linguistic programming taught me that if I emulated my interlocutor's body and verbal language, I could be more effective in achieving my goals. That's also what code-switching is about. One day, I decided to give it a try with my boss. He barely gestured when he spoke, so I started doing the same. He talked in short sentences, so I communicated the same way. His expressions were not very effusive, so I tried being direct and neutral in my communication. It worked incredibly well.

As one of my spiritual teachers says, «Use everything, absolutely everything, for your growth and advancement.» Let's make peace with code switching, knowing that we are not changing our essence. Start by interacting with your audience in the way that works the best for you to achieve your goals.

SLOWLY TURN UP YOUR VOLUME

Kat Vera, a young Latina engineer at Pfizer, introduced me to this metaphor of her creation.

—Little by little, I turned up the volume —she told me—. I was never fake or inauthentic, but Kat at volume 15 differs from Kat at volume 50 and, in turn, at volume 75.

When we talk about volume, we are not referring to the volume of our voice but to the totality of our expression, including our way of speaking, the rhythm and tone of voice, the movement of our hands, and the emphasis and passion we use when communicating. This strategy is ideal when you find yourself in spaces where people don't fully know you, whether it's a new job, a new project within your organization, or in front of a group of people with whom you don't interact frequently. Remember when I suggested bringing your light gradually so as not to dazzle those not used to the special and unique sparkle you emit? Well, that's precisely what this is about.

—If my passion and drive are considered too aggressive, it's up to me to manage that perception that people may have of me. Not for them, but because it's what's the best for my career at the moment —Kat told me—. I know myself. I like showing my passion and ambition and being brave and direct. But I had to learn to do it in such a way that people would listen to me so that I could be effective in my work.

ACT OF HEALTHY REBELLION

Think about two different work relationships: one that works well and another that could improve. Analyze:

Do I exhibit different volumes in each of these relationships? How can I temporarily adjust my volume to improve the relationship that doesn't work quite well?

_____
_____
_____
_____

Kat learned to read her audience. Over time, she realized that she could gradually turn up the volume with the same person or keep it steady if that was the best for her goals.

—Some people don't want volume 80 at work and feel uncomfortable with that. So, if I want to be effective with them, I must express myself at a volume they can handle —she told me, and wisely added—: Having the emotional intelligence to read my audience and know what volume to use makes me feel empowered. I remind myself that I am confidently and intentionally leading my professional life.

I hope these stories guide you as you seek to find your way of showing up and using your voice. I invite you to experiment with these techniques, which do not seek to change your authenticity and essence but open up spaces and opportunities for diverse self-expression. Ironically, there is no greater freedom than allowing yourself to be who you need to be in the circumstances you face. Nothing is more limiting than trying to impose a single way of being and expression to the changing environments around you.

I dream of the day we are valued for who we are beyond how we sound, look, and show up. We are not there yet, so it is up to us to experiment with these tools to continue moving forward with our professional goals.

STILL FEEL LIKE AN IMPOSTOR?

Before closing this chapter, I want to touch on the so-called impostor syndrome, although it's a term I don't use frequently. It describes the experience of those who don't feel part of an environment and feel anxiety about being exposed as a fraud.

A 2021 article by Tulshyan and Burey explains why using «impostor syndrome» to describe that experience is inappropriate. When we talk about a syndrome, we put the burden on women to overcome what sounds like a pathology instead of focusing on where the problem lies: that women, particularly women of color, face systemic obstacles to our professional growth.

What needs to be fixed is not an emotional pathology but the inequities in hiring, promoting, developing, and compensating women that currently place us at a disadvantage. Think about the original creators of corporate cultures and those who dominated entrepreneurial spaces before women and people of color were admitted into them. It's normal to feel uncomfortable in an environment not created with our growth and success in mind. There's nothing wrong with you. You were created perfect and complete. Reconnect with your authentic essence and shatter all the false messages of lack and insufficiency that the world made you believe.

As Reshma Saujani, activist and founder of Girls Who Code, said during a commencement speech at Smith College, «The problem and the solution are bigger than any of us. It's not your job to change who you are, but it is your job to change the system.»

LESSONS LEARNED

- Millions of us were taught to stay silent, particularly in ambiguous, conflicting, or uncomfortable situations. The problem is that those who don't speak lose in our workspaces.

- Speaking confidently about yourself requires you to be your number one fan. This will give you the strength to show who you are and ask for what you deserve. Loving yourself unconditionally is a decision you can make today.

- Before speaking, remember the acronym WAIT: **Why Am I T**alking? Remember the importance of knowing your audience and acting strategically toward what you want to achieve with them.

- Building your professional brand and expressing yourself authentically is not about having the loudest voice in the room but about contributing what you and only you can bring to the conversation: your point of differentiation.

- We can use code switching as a flexible tool that allows us to temporarily adapt to the environment to reach our audience without changing our true essence.

- The so-called impostor syndrome puts the burden of what sounds like a pathology on our shoulders instead of focusing on the systemic obstacles and inequities that hinder our growth.

CHAPTER 9

Dare to go for more

What does *going for more* mean for you? In what area of your life do you feel a calling to achieve something even greater? Listen to your heart. Refrain from minimizing the voice of intuition that wants to show you the way. Remember that your biggest dreams can speak to you in whispers. So, ask yourself: What is it that I long for?

Immediately after I arrived in the United States, I started to deny myself the opportunity to dream big. My heart showed me what I longed for, my biggest aspirations and desires, yet the inner voices were too loud and overpowering, howling *Women like you don't achieve that*; *It's impossible, how are you going to do it?*; *You don't have the money or the time*; *You don't have the connections*. My tendency to self-sabotage and take me out of the race before I even started increased exponentially in the land of the American dream, which I find ironic. How did that happen?

It was not always like that. In my native Argentina, with considerably fewer resources and opportunities than in the United States, I witnessed my parents dream big, particularly regarding my siblings and me and our education. I heard them proudly affirm I would be the first woman in my family to go to college, a space utterly unknown to them. Never, not even once, did they hesitate that I would achieve that ambitious goal; even though we lived in a small town removed from Buenos Aires, our financial situation could not afford such an investment, and there wasn't one single person in our extended family who had ever achieved that goal. Anyone would say that we had more headwinds than tailwinds. Yet, my parents persisted in holding that vision, so I embraced it as mine and made it a reality.

Years later, and once in the United States, my experience was quite different. Feeling like a foreigner and out of place, labeled as different, and struggling with my fear of letting myself down, I settled for pocket-sized dreams, which are scaled-down versions of the real thing.

But my hunger for meaning and purpose was still there, and it started to become a stronger itch that challenged me to dare to pursue those dreams that seemed out of my reach. To get myself back on the path, I had to rummage through my trunk of memories until I found that powerful trait I had observed in my parents the ability to create a vision of what I want and to start walking towards it, even when I don't know exactly how to get there and when I know I will face multiple challenges on my way.

Before we keep going, close your eyes and open your hands, mind, and heart to accept this gift that my parents left for me and that today I want it to be yours as well: allow yourself to create a vision of what you long for and believe it possible. Promise yourself you will start walking towards it now, no matter how few resources, connections, or talents you think you possess. Will you accept this gift?

SELF-DOUBT AND TRAUMA BLOCK OUR ADVANCEMENT: AN ANCESTRAL LEGACY?

How often do we create a vision of what we want, only to abandon it later, allowing voices of self-doubt to push us to give up? *Am I doing it right? Do I have what it takes to succeed? Will I meet my expectations and those of others? Can I succeed in this space where I feel I don't belong?*

Many times, that self-doubt shows up when we look at ourselves in .the mirror that spaces of power hold in front of us, and in which we don't find ourselves reflected. Feeling somehow different makes us doubt ourselves even more. I learned that self-doubt may become so ingrained in our unconscious thinking that we pass it down to younger generations without realizing it.

Alice Rodriguez has firsthand experience on how this works. She was born in the United States in an ancestral line of very strong women. Her maternal grandmother, mother of 12 children, did not know how to read or write. After becoming a widow in Mexico, her home country, she made the difficult decision to send several of her children to live with other relatives to make ends meet.

—My mom was amazing —Alice told me—. She arrived here at 15 years old without knowing a word of English and with a sixth-grade education at best, but with the desire and drive to get ahead, even when her opportunities were limited.

With this determination to advance, each generation moved a little further ahead. Alice was the first in her family to complete her university studies. She excelled for 35 years at JPMorgan, holding leadership positions in several cities nationwide.

—I always wanted to go further than my ancestors since I witnessed all that my mother sacrificed to give me a better future —Alice continued—. Several times, I thought life was unfair, especially because some had so much and others so little. However, I learned not to waste energy complaining and to direct it towards moving forward.

Like many of us pioneers in our spaces, Alice had moments when she felt different and doubted herself. When that happened, she drew strength from within to keep moving towards her goals. She never imagined that her daughters, born in Texas in environments very different from where Alice grew up and removed from the immigration process of their ancestors, could carry similar doubts to those she had faced. She realized that the feeling of not belonging and our self-doubts can be perpetuated over time, even among subsequent generations born and raised in this country.

—My daughter, who had been admitted to a prestigious medical school, told me she sometimes felt out of place. She felt that she didn't fit in culturally and began to doubt her abilities —Alice shared—. It hurt me to realize that younger generations are also affected, carrying the heavy cultural baggage of doubt and lack of belonging—. About two hundred students were in her daughter's medical school graduating class, of which only 12 were Latino. It was natural for her to feel somewhat out of place, but her reaction was unexpected for Alice.

The difficulties faced by our ancestors, combined with the trauma of immigration and acculturation, impact that generation and are transferred to subsequent generations. Some time ago, Psychology Today magazine published an article explaining the existence of *psychic legacies* perpetuated through unconscious signals or messages that flow between the adult and the child.

It is normal to feel that our ancestors' struggles still influence us as we carry them in our DNA. It is expected that those of us who come from a culture that has historically been deemed inferior will continue to doubt our abilities and feel out of place. My question is: now that we know these influences are real and can limit us, how can we confidently pursue our dreams and ambitions? Doubt is neither neutral nor harmless. Doubt wears down, erodes, paralyzes, and sickens our minds. Doubt consumes energy, which we could better channel towards achieving our dreams and goals. Despite all the internal work I've done in recent years, I live plagued with doubts. However, I no longer try to hide them under the rug because when I've done that, they come back with full force. I simply embrace them, bless them, thank them for trying to protect me, and assure them that everything will be fine. We come from ancestors with admirable inner strength. Let us remember where we come from to leap where we are going.

YOU NO LONGER NEED TO BE THE GOOD GIRL

Not only do we doubt ourselves and feel out of place, but we can also carry the unconscious mandate to be the good girl who doesn't break the rules. Following this mandate has a clear consequence: we limit our potential and let opportunities and money pass us by. I mentioned earlier in the book that research indicates that men apply for jobs only when they meet 60% of the requirements, while women only apply if they meet 100%. In other words, women are left behind when going after bigger and better opportunities.

Tara Mohr, author of Playing Big, dedicated herself to thoroughly understanding this phenomenon. In the past, it had been argued that women let opportunities pass because of our self-doubt. But Tara discovered something deeper: 78% of the women who participated in her study expressed that they had not pursued those more significant and better opportunities because they believed they had to meet 100% of the requirements to apply. In other words, these women thought the requirements were inflexible, and because of that, they refrained from applying as they wanted to follow the rules. They were taking the requirements more seriously than men.

From childhood, girls are socialized to follow the rules, and we are rewarded or praised when we demonstrate obedience. *Good girls sit this way; Good girls don't talk back; Good girls remain silent while adults talk; Good girls help with household chores.* Boys are allowed more space for rebellion. *Boys are active and can't sit still; Boys are like that: they play rough.* And how about the assertive girl judged as bossy, while a boy is considered a leader for that same behavior? We cling so tightly to the good girl cultural mandate that we keep dragging it into our

> **ACT OF HEALTHY REBELLION**
>
> **Reflect:**
>
> *In what circumstances did being the good girl work against me? Have I missed job opportunities, projects, or earning more money? Have I silenced myself, settling for less than I deserve? Did I convince myself that it's better not to ask for more?*
>
> _____
>
> _____
>
> _____
>
> _____
>
> _____
>
> **Let's break through this habit together.**

adult lives, perhaps to feel the acceptance, love, and support we may have lacked during childhood. Then we have a problem when the fear of being judged as *bad girls* takes us out of the race before we even start running it.

STEPS TO DARE TO GO FOR MORE

Up to this point, we have discussed the importance of having a vision of what we want, even when we don't have the resources we think we need to manifest it. We have also discussed how self-doubt and the good girl mandate can get in the way. In the following pages, I will offer you a roadmap to ask for what you want and negotiate with confidence.

Step 1: Start with your mindset

If, as a child, you were told that you asked for too much *(How demanding! How greedy!)*, it's possible that today, you hold yourself back before asking for what you want. Something similar can happen if you unconsciously embrace the role of caregiver, the one who takes care of everyone without asking for anything in return. I had to unlearn the ingrained belief that by working very hard and being perfect, the rewards would come without me asking for them. I focused on working very hard, rarely stepping out of my comfort zone to ask for what I wanted. As a result, I went seven years without a salary increase, and later on, as a business owner, I accepted meager prices from my clients without sitting down to negotiate with them.

ACT OF HEALTHY REBELLION

Think about the specific words you heard when you asked something from authority figures in your life:

Was I told that I was asking for too much? Was I told that I was greedy or selfish or that it was not okay for me to ask? Was I humiliated when asking? Did I feel guilt or shame? Did I feel rejected and stopped trying?

_____

_____

_____

_____

Words you heard in your past may have become the inner voice that now holds you back when asking. It's possible that the same emotions you felt back then, such as guilt or shame, continue to show up when you make your ask. As you now know, if we become aware of what we think and how we feel, we can begin to change it.

> **ACT OF HEALTHY REBELLION**
>
> *Let's do the same exercise,*
> *but this time specifically with money:*
>
> ¿What messages did I receive about money? Was I told that it was dirty, that it changed people's essence, attracted the wrong crowds, or that those with money earned it by hurting others? Was I told that making a lot of money is impossible if my mission is to help others?
>
> _____
>
> _____
>
> _____
>
> _____

Can you see why asking for money, resources, or support might be difficult? On the one hand, you want to earn more money, and you are aware of the advantages of having more wealth, but on the other hand, you possibly grew up thinking that money corrupts, divides families, or comes at the cost of enormous sacrifices. You may be carrying an internal dilemma. One part of you wants more, but the other subconsciously repels it. And this inner interference can make you sound insecure when making your ask.

Step 2: Understand where you are and the alternatives ahead

Write down your strengths and success stories

Remember the work we did on your values and the characteristics of your personal brand? When it comes to asking and negotiating, it's important to remember your strengths and what makes you a valuable professional. Write down every success story you achieved inside and outside your organization. Take notes of projects completed ahead of schedule, results that exceeded expectations, connections you established that ended in strategic alliances, courses and certifications you completed, philanthropic activities you are involved in, and boards where you are serving. Take notes of all this now to have the information at hand when you most need it.

Those of us who are multicultural and navigate two worlds and two value systems must remind ourselves more often of our unique strengths and abilities. When I need a boost of confidence and self-esteem, I visualize the dust-filled streets of my hometown and everything I accomplished to get to where I am. It was not easy at all, but I did it.

You are a natural leader. If you don't believe me, consider that there is no way you could have gotten this far without being a leader and pioneer, making your way into the unknown. Observe the journeys and experiences of your ancestors as well. Their resilience to keep moving forward past significant obstacles runs in your veins, even if you don't fully acknowledge it. We are resilient, courageous, daring, loyal, dreamers, hard workers, and natural negotiators. Those skills are the leadership qualities that will transform this country and the world. Let's give them value.

Work on your areas of opportunity

Being honest with our weaknesses, or as I prefer to call them, our areas of opportunity is not always easy. Science has shown that humans have blind spots that prevent us from seeing in full transparency what may cause us to feel uncomfortable or ashamed of ourselves. It is OK to feel uncomfortable with our weaknesses. But if we push them aside and avoid taking an honest look into our weak points, we risk being blocked by them. That is why it's so important to be aware of your areas of opportunity and to have a proactive plan to keep working on those areas.

Logic would indicate that if we ask for feedback from those around us, we will better see what others see. It's not that easy. There are many studies, including one that Textio ran with 25,000 participants, that indicate that women, particularly women of color, do not receive clear and complete feedback but rather superficial information that does not help us. Textio analyzed the type of feedback that different ethnic and racial groups receive in the United States and found that Latina women receive the least clear feedback. We are left wondering what exactly we need to change or improve. Every single Latina woman in the survey said she received feedback that had to do with how others perceive her personality (*You're too emotional!* or *You have a lot of opinions*) and not with the quality of her work, compared to 75% for white men, who also said they do get comments on their personality, but ones that praise their way of being (*You show a lot of confidence and ambition*). Regarding actionable feedback or tangible examples to understand what we could change, Latina women receive half that type of feedback compared to white men.

That's why we need to make an additional effort with our bosses, colleagues, and clients and specifically ask for tangible examples, sometimes assuring them that we won't take it personally, and explaining their feedback is vital to our professional growth.

We need to know exactly where to focus our efforts to keep growing. Make it a habit to ask for micro-feedback sessions. Since we need tangible examples to make effective adjustments, the best time to ask for that feedback is immediately after a particular event. Don't wait for too long. Also, make sure you create an action plan to improve each area. For example, if they tell you that they expect you to contribute more ideas in meetings or to complete a project in less time, make sure to make those changes immediately and then ask for additional feedback («*How do you think I'm progressing with your suggestions?*»).

Next time you ask for what you want or need, keep your strengths and progress in your areas of opportunity at hand. Work on your improvement plan even before you are asked to do so, and in the process, request continuous feedback with specific and clear examples.

Step 3: Establish your non-negotiables

When I brought the Rising Together movement to Boston, we presented a panel in which Dr. Gail Ayala Taylor explained how defining her non-negotiable terms had helped her negotiate for what she wanted.

—Help me understand all this about non-negotiables —I asked her when we were alone at the end of the event—. I find I establish my non-negotiables and then change them —I confessed. During several negotiations, I gave in, usually working more and earning less.

Dr. Gail Ayala Taylor is one of the women I admire the most. She is a professor at Dartmouth College, where I pursued my master's degree, although we met several years later. A mother of four children, she is also the founder of the organization RISE, a platform that supports women in successfully transitioning into their early careers.

—If you change them, they are not non-negotiables, but instead boundaries that you are flexing according to the circumstances —she explained—. A non-negotiable is precisely that: it's something you do not negotiate. My non-negotiables do not change because if they do, I know I will negatively impact my life or my loved ones.

Gail asked me to imagine my non-negotiables as a box with rigid edges.

—Be careful with what you place in that box because those walls are rigid. If you try to bend them, which is equivalent to giving in on your non-negotiables, you can break them, and with that, you can impact your self-confidence by breaking an agreement you had with yourself.

On the other hand, the box walls where we place our boundaries are soft. This gives us the flexibility to modify those boundaries according to the circumstances and then put them back in place. Flexing them continuously can eventually break them, too, so we must also try to keep those soft boundaries in place.

—Working in an industry that doesn't seem to align with my values would be a non-negotiable for me. So, no matter how much money or opportunities they offer me, my involvement in those spaces is not negotiated. Let me offer you another example —Gail continued—: due to my demanding family life, I do my best to schedule my meetings from Monday to Thursday and reserve Fridays for thinking, writing, or studying. This is a boundary because I flex my boundaries if I have to meet with someone who is busy and only available on a Friday. The same goes if you have the boundary of not working on weekends. You may have an important presentation on a Monday and need to prepare for it. So, you can adjust that boundary for that weekend and then put it back in place.

> **ACT OF HEALTHY REBELLION**
>
> ***Think about a dream opportunity you have wanted to ask for, and get ready to negotiate.***
>
> Create two lists: one with your non-negotiables and another with your boundaries.
>
> _____   _____
>
> _____   _____
>
> _____   _____
>
> _____   _____
>
> _____   _____
>
> For example, if you ask for more money, have a range of values. The upper amount should make you feel slightly uncomfortable because of how high it is, while the lower value should be the minimum you are willing to do the work for. The upper amount can be a boundary (flexible), and the lower amount can be your non-negotiable.

Step 4: Make your ask!

So far, you worked on your inner dialogue and mindset. You also made a list of your strengths and areas of opportunity, as well as your boundaries and non-negotiables. Now it's time to ask, but how?

When great negotiators present their case and ask for money, they mention their desired amount and then remain silent. They don't say another word. In that silence, they create space for the other party to react, even if it's uncomfortable. This space is sacred, and if you learn to use it, it gives you the power and shows that you have confidence in yourself and know what you want. After going seven years without a salary increase, I did the opposite of remaining silent the day I sat down to negotiate. I presented my case and mentioned my desired amount, but I continued offering justifications and explanations that started to sound like a ramble. I ended up entangling in my own words, stumbling and nervous. My voice of self-judgment came back in full force, and it goes without saying that I didn't receive the money I was asking for.

So now you know: present your case showing facts and statistics if you have them, make your ask, and... silence. Let the other party accept your offer or present you with a counteroffer. If they offer you an amount that doesn't feel right, you can ask for some time to consider it. Don't make a rushed decision under pressure; don't give in if you don't feel sure.

When it does not work as planned

For too long, I associated the money I earned with my worth and value. Because of this, I took the many rejections I faced along the way as direct rejections of me as a person. As a business owner, I'm still working on this. I tend to get tangled up when it comes to separating my worth and human value from my business income, and more than once, my fear of rejection gets in the way of me asking for more. Latina women need to keep asking, and when faced with a *no*, we need to negotiate.

A Mexican immigrant and the first in her family to attend college, Claudia began her journey working at McDonald's as a cashier and in the kitchen to pay for her studies. She later transitioned to the insurance industry. Claudia attended community college while working full-time, graduated at 30, and found herself balancing multiple professional and maternal demands when her first baby was born.

Along her professional path, Claudia encountered many *nos* but never gave up. Her career continued to grow until she reached a director position, where, despite being one of the few Latina women in that role, she set her goal to be promoted to vice president. And guess what? Claudia applied seven times for a VP position, which was given to someone else each time.

—How did you keep trying when you possibly wanted to give up? —was my first question for Claudia.

—I'm human, and it wasn't easy —she said—. Each time I got a *no*, I would spend the first day feeling sorry for myself, questioning my worth, and feeling a victim with limited talents. I gave myself space to feel all that frustration for one day. The next day, I would pivot my thinking. I would tell myself that, for some reason, that particular position wasn't meant for me and that something better would come along. On the third day, I would take action, doing the work I knew I would do well and focused on creating impact from my place while staying alert to the next opportunity.

Claudia's attitude deserves admiration. She accepted her situation without giving up, throwing it all away, or feeling sorry for herself for days without end. By fully accepting what had happened, she could see her reality with neutrality and inner peace, even if she didn't entirely like it.

There were days when Claudia would tell herself:

—«Maybe this is as far as I've come, and if so, I accept it. It's been a long journey already,» but a little voice inside me kept telling me that I deserved that promotion, that I should keep trying —she would ask herself—: «Look, what if next time you don't apply out of fear or reluctance, and that was your opportunity?»

The little voice in her heart won. On the eighth opportunity and feeling she had nothing to lose, Claudia showed up to her interviews more relaxed, with more self-confidence, and knowing that she didn't need that external validation to know her worth. On that eighth opportunity, Claudia was promoted to vice president.

—My strength and resilience come from a very personal place —she told me—. I lived in Tijuana, Baja California, as a teenager and studied in San Diego. My mom would drop me off at the border daily, and I had to walk two miles in the rain or heat. Can you imagine? At that time, there were no cell phones, so I was cut off from my family during the journey. I would tell myself on those long walks: «This is temporary. This will pass. This is only for some time, and something very good will result from this.» —That is the same dialogue that today, as an adult, I keep repeating in my mind: «I will keep walking without giving up. These difficult situations are only temporary.»

There is much to learn from Claudia's story: her hope, resilience, and the fact that she did not give up when that little voice told her to keep going. I know from experience that rejection hurts and leaves a mark and that, over time, the accumulation of rejections can bring us down. The only way we can keep moving forward is by making the vision of what we want larger and stronger than the rejection we will encounter along the way.

At some point, it's also valid to say, «This is as far as I've come with this,» if you really feel that way. It's perfectly fine for that to be the case. Make sure it's your heart talking and not your wounded ego. Your ego will speak from anger or pain, while the heart will do so from a place of total acceptance. If it's your heart talking, you will notice the knot in your stomach loosen up, your shoulders will release the tension you carried for so long, and a very deep part of you will come to appreciate the beauty of the ephemeral of what is now gone. You will experience peace and gratitude for what was not possible in your life.

In my mission to support the advancement of our community, I encountered many dead ends and doors that did not want to open. With my discipline, drive, perseverance (and maybe a little stubbornness!) I kept pushing hard against those doors, causing myself more pain with each rejection, until the accumulation of emotional pain transformed into a physical imbalance that prevented me from working for several months. I thought about giving up and dropping it all off, but the calling in my heart was stronger. I had to learn to accept that particular doors will not open, tell myself that perhaps others more aligned with my purpose are waiting behind other doors, and that what shows up in our lives is not always exactly as we would like it to be.

Your journey toward achieving more will present you with challenging moments where you will face the dilemma of either holding onto what has been central to your life or letting it go to create space for new opportunities. If you become attached to what was supposed to take place in your life, it is possible that the decision to let it go will not be easy at all. But in the same way as there are moments to ask, there are moments to insist and negotiate, and there are also moments to let go. Only your heart knows what is best for you.

Let's set aside the judgments we hold against ourselves when asking for support, resources, or money. Money and other material objects are neither good nor bad; they simply *are*. We are the ones who give them meaning. The problem arises when we transform money and other material objects into a crutch for our lack of self-esteem or when we hope the material will quench our insatiable thirst for power for the sake of power. That is why, I will insist, the world needs more power and money in the hands of conscious human beings whose mission is to leave the world better than they found it.

LESSONS LEARNED

- Many of us who are immigrants with a successful career in our home countries face so many doubts, prejudices, and barriers in the United States that, over time, we may stop daring to dream big.

- Just as our trauma is passed down from generation to generation, self-doubt and lack of belonging, also known as psychic legacies, are heavy cultural burdens that we also pass on to our children.

- We have been led to be the good girl who doesn't break the rules and only goes after an opportunity when she meets 100% of the requirements. This deprives us of greater growth and more money in our lives.

- We have culturally assigned money a negative connotation, perhaps because our ancestors had a survival relationship with it. On the one hand, we want to earn more, but on the other, our subconscious tells us that the consequences of attracting more money into our lives could be negative.

- In the adventure of going for more, we may encounter several doors that do not open. It is up to us to discern whether to continue insisting or accept that particular doors will not open for us and that they could indicate that other opportunities more aligned with our purpose are awaiting elsewhere.

- We must learn to ask for support, resources, and money. Money and other material things are neither good nor bad; they just are. The problem lies in transforming the material into a crutch for our lack of self-esteem. Go for more! The world needs more money, power, and influence in the hands of people with conscious values like you.

PART III

Master Your Game

CHAPTER 10

From one to many, a turning point

For those of us who grew up without imagining that one day we would be leaders, the transition from having nobody reporting to us or from being a solopreneur (as they call entrepreneurs who do not yet have employees) to leading a team of people reporting to us is a significant turning point. Perhaps the most difficult part is pivoting our mindsets and belief systems as we continue to grow in our profession.

This stage allows you to embrace your role as a change agent and multiply your impact. What better opportunity than to create your microcosm within your team: a platform with gender equality, respect for all voices, and a psychologically safe space for everyone to contribute their best? You now have the chance to replicate all the great things your previous bosses taught you and learn from those situations that seemed unfair to do things differently now that you are in charge. That is being an actual change agent.

Becoming a team leader is not that accessible for women. According to the «Women in the Workplace» study by Lean In and McKinsey & Co., the main barrier for women is not just the glass ceiling, defined as the obstacles we face in getting to executive positions. Our obstacles appear much earlier, with what the report describes as the broken rung. This term illustrates that for every 100 men promoted to team leaders, only 87 women are also promoted. And when it comes to women of color, only 73 are promoted. The «broken rung» signals that we fall behind early on.

Something similar happens with business owners. Census numbers show that almost 75% of businesses in the United States have no employees. They are solopreneurs. If we add up the sales generated by these businesses, that figure accounts for just 4% of the total sales from all companies in the country. In other words, many business owners continue to work alone, generating minimal sales. Barriers such as access to the latest technology and tools, access to capital, and lack of contract opportunities with corporations and other large organizations are some of the many hurdles we face in expanding our businesses.

Therefore, consider that having a team reporting to you is a success. In this chapter, I will provide you with the tools you need to succeed at this stage, whether you are a new leader or an experienced supervisor or manager.

YOUR SUCCESS IS NO LONGER JUST YOURS

—Going from having no staff to managing others and being responsible for them was a big step for me —Lisa, the Latina executive in the health industry whom I introduced to you earlier, told me— and I think the higher your workplace performance is without direct reports, the harder this transition can be.

Her words resonated deeply. What was most difficult for me was to let go of the need to control every detail, which, up to the point of becoming a manager, had helped me build my profile as high-potential in the organization. Out of the fear of feeling humiliated in public or being judged for my team's output if that was not satisfactory, I took refuge in the safety of knowing all the details related to my work.

—The more you grow, the more you need to allow team members to do things you don't know exactly how to do —Lisa assured me—. That can be uncomfortable unless you accept that you no longer need to be on top of all the detailed work yourself but rather direct your team towards a common vision without competing with them or proving you know as much as they do or more.

Competition. Insecurities. Need for control. They all seem to direct us to look at the inner voices and belief systems that hide behind these traits, which can get in our way as leaders of others.

THE INNER VOICES THAT IMPACT OUR LEADERSHIP STYLE

In our subconscious, we will find once again outdated thought patterns that can no longer accompany us on the path ahead. Let's cover together the gender roles that affect us when it comes to taking leadership positions, our relationship with the concept of authority and, lastly, the habit of doing it alone and stoically. Let's go step by step.

Leader, me?

In our Latin American culture, it has been historically uncommon to find women in positions of power within the Church, the government, the military, and agricultural spaces. Generally, these areas that concentrate great power in the countries we come from are led mainly by men. Our role in those spaces has been secondary, more like the role of someone who supports the leadership and agendas of others.

«I felt totally inadequate and intimidated by my role as a leader,» several women told me, most of them high executives in their organizations or successful businesswomen who had scaled up their ventures as if defying the statistics that say that we rarely grow beyond $250,000 in annual revenue.

Finding ourselves at the head of the table is not our natural cultural role. It is not the one that has been implanted in our mindsets for centuries and, very possibly, not the one we learned within our family because our mothers and grandmothers did not always have access to the opportunities we now have. Many of us have been influenced to follow the white, non-Latino, male leadership model, or that is all we have known. That style may feel foreign to our most natural leadership ways and leave us exhausted as we keep pushing ourselves to manage others in ways that do not work for us. It is like trying to fit into shoes that are not your size.

To become an effective leader, first, you must create that image within yourself. Remember the visualization strategy I talked about in previous chapters? Imagine yourself in great detail sitting at the table confidently, feeling valued and respected by the rest of the team. Simultaneously, create an inner dialogue that empowers you and lets go of the voices of judgment that want to bring you down. Support your success from within. Win in your imagination. Finally, remember that if you have reached this leadership role despite the «broken rung,» you have already overcome one of the first significant obstacles. Let this build your confidence, and believe you have what it takes to grow.

Nobody does it like me

Delegating is a trust exercise where you give others the freedom and space to do their work, develop their character, increase their self-confidence, and work on their own beliefs and self-imposed barriers. A problem for us and our teams is when we believe no one else can do it like us. And if you think that, you are right. At least initially, others will not do the work as quickly or as well as you can, either because you've done it for a longer time or because you acquired skills that others are still working on.

There is more. Those of us who are the first generation in our families to become managers or hire employees for our business are used to paving our way practically by ourselves. We have done it all our lives. Simply put, we had no one to ask for help, or we were too embarrassed to show we did not know how to solve a problem lest they realize we were «impostors.» We got used to fighting our battles in loneliness, often carrying the entire world on our shoulders. As leaders, we need to unlearn the cultural script that says we must do everything ourselves and learn from those who have walked this path before.

—As a leader, you can build a team culture where people feel safe to experiment, fail, learn from their mistakes, and grow —Lisa told me—. Being a leader is not about giving them a list of tasks and disappearing, nor about looking over the other person's shoulder and controlling them at every step. Being a leader involves the art of finding balance. It is about setting clear goals, explaining what you expect from each person, coordinating to meet with them regularly, and insisting they can come to you whenever they need your support or have questions. To start, at a minimum, delegate the tasks required by their role. And then see if you can add more. In the long run, you want to give them exposure so that they showcase their work to executives or clients, even if their voice trembles a bit. That's how they will grow, by feeling a bit uncomfortable.

Lisa told me she noticed several times that the manager delegating the tasks tends to get more nervous than the person presenting to executives or clients, especially when the delegating manager feels that there is a lot at stake, including their image as a leader.

—I remember when I had to give an important presentation to hundreds of people —Lisa told me—. While I was presenting, I could see my boss nervously walking back and forth at the back of the room in an attempt to control his nerves.

That wasn't the only time. On a second occasion, one of her bosses was furiously biting his nails while sitting in the front row as she presented her work.

—As a leader, make sure to be a supportive face in the audience, and not a figure that spreads insecurity and fear —Lisa recommended—. As parents feel that our children go out into the world representing us and our values, we may feel the same when a team member gets exposure and visibility. So, if you ever find yourself in this situation, remember to stay calm!

ACT OF HEALTHY REBELLION

Reflect on your limiting beliefs around delegation. Write:

What am I afraid of when I refuse to give up control?

_____

_____

_____

_____

When deciding what to delegate, remember that just because you can do something does not mean you should do it. You have the power to choose.

They don't respect my authority

If you expect people to respect your authority in the workplace like we were taught to respect it at home, you will suffer a lot! Our culture instilled respect towards elders and authority figures, sometimes enforcing it via «la chancla.» We learned not to question those we perceived as authority, as we knew the consequence of our questioning could end in punishment. In Anglo-Saxon culture, we find quite the opposite: children develop their voices early on and are not afraid to question authority.

Later on, we encounter similar behaviors in the workplace. In the United States, you are expected to present your point of view, even when it is different from the point of view of those who hold a position of authority. The theory behind this practice is that if everyone contributes their point of view, even when divergent, that collective input can improve the final product. Divergent points of view can be good for business.

Because of these cultural differences, it may be uncomfortable when a team member publicly questions our way of thinking, particularly if that happens in front of executives or our clients. I have been through those situations, when the slightest questioning of my thinking or conclusions made me so uncomfortable I felt humiliated and blushed intensely. I would feel out of place, lose my train of thought, and retreat into silence.

For anyone aspiring to continue growing as a leader, a fundamental key when you are questioned is never to take it personally. Of course, we are talking about reasonable questioning and not disrespect. We do not have to tolerate disrespect.

—I incorporated the habit of gathering my team in one room to share my ideas with them and ask for their input. I insisted that they tell me what they thought with total transparency —Lisa explained. In her early career years, she felt uncomfortable with some of the comments she received during these meetings. Still, over time, she understood the enormous advantage of asking for others' opinions. Meeting with her team was very beneficial for her, as everyone could say what they thought in a private space and not blurt it out unexpectedly in a meeting with executives or clients.

At the end of our meeting, Lisa told me that she follows a work-with-me approach to being an effective leader. With it, Lisa creates spaces where all voices are heard and where there

> **ACT OF HEALTHY REBELLION**
>
> ***Think about your last interaction where your authority was challenged. Answer:***
>
> *How did I react? Did cultural differences play a role? What could I have done differently? What will I do differently from now on to create spaces for healthy divergence and disagreement?*
>
> _____
>
> _____
>
> _____
>
> _____

is room for all to grow. I call that *leadership of the new era*: a leadership style that we, as change agents immersed in a system with so much room for improvement, are invited to implement. Being a conscious team leader is a great way to be a change agent.

Now that we have explored the main cultural mindsets that can hinder your success as a leader, let's examine three fundamental pillars that you should consider when building a high-performing team.

Pillar 1: Understand your team's motivations

Just as I strive to stay connected with what energizes and commits me to my work, I also seek to understand what motivates those who report to me and even those who report to them. This requires investing time with each individual and asking questions to understand who they are and their core motivations.

- *What is your professional background? How was your journey to get here?*
- *How do you define success in your professional career? What do you want from your profession?*
- *How do you see yourself in three years? And in five or ten years?*
- *What motivates you to get up every morning and show up to work? Why?*

In this last question, you can continue asking «why?» three or four times until you reach the deepest motivation for that person. At first, their answers may be related to growing in their profession or saving for their future, but if you dig a little deeper, more profound motivations may emerge, such as feeling part of a team that creates an impact on others' lives, feeling valued and accepted, or being acknowledged for a job well done. It will be different for each person. Knowing your team at this deeper level will set the basis for stronger relationships, which can positively impact your team's performance and benefit your image as a leader.

Achieving this closeness within a team is especially important with younger team members. In the United States, almost half of the workforce today comprises millennials and Generation Z. According to a Gallup study, these individuals prefer to find in their bosses a mentor or coach who helps them grow rather than only a boss who merely delegates tasks to them. New generations seek a sense of purpose and want to know they are contributing to a mission of impact. They value formal and informal conversations, showing genuine interest in who they are. They respect bosses who display their authentic selves and motivate them to give their best and be productive. In other words, young talent is moved by authentic, less hierarchical relationships and greater closeness with their managers.

This is where our cultural ability to connect with other human beings and to be empathetic, warm, and human comes in handy as we lead, develop, and motivate the workforce of tomorrow.

Pillar 2: Learn to be comfortable giving uncomfortable feedback

Giving feedback to others, especially the kind of feedback that pinpoints areas of opportunity, can be pretty uncomfortable for both parties, whether we find ourselves delivering the *bad news* or as its recipients.

This discomfort has its roots in our cultural *simpatía*, a script that influences us to maintain harmonious relationships with others. If we think our words can create a conflict, we may tend to remain silent, as we may also do if we fear hurting others out of how much we usually care about them. Beyond how uncomfortable you may feel giving feedback to your team, this practice is a key pillar for their advancement and to develop them into a high-performing team. Because all human beings have blind spots that prevent us from being objective with ourselves, feedback becomes key to continuously adjusting the team's actions and achieving a more significant collective impact.

The first step is to pivot the meaning of feedback we hold in our minds, shifting from seeing it as a necessary evil to seeing it as a way to help others. Reframe the act of giving feedback as a great gift you give to others to support their growth. The second step is to utilize a proven roadmap to provide assertive and valuable feedback. Here is mine:

1. THANK. Express your gratitude for their time and for the work they did. This will open people's hearts so they receive your feedback more openly, helping disarm defensiveness.
2. ASK. Before giving your point of view, ask, «How do you think the meeting went (referring to a specific meeting)?» Listen carefully. This is where any blind spots your team member has may show up.
3. EXPLAIN. Provide tangible examples of what could have been done better. Remember that multicultural individuals generally receive unspecific feedback. Break this systemic habit!
4. RECOMMEND. Offer possible courses of action: «How about next time you try…?»
5. MOTIVATE. Help them understand how the new behavior will benefit them and the organization. Make sure to state the benefit, as humans modify their behavior only when we understand the benefit.
6. CLARIFY. Leave some time to clarify doubts: «Do you have any questions?»
7. OFFER. Close by offering your support, becoming a mentor or coach rather than just a boss. You can ask: «How can I continue to support your growth?»

To continue supporting a change in behavior, make sure to acknowledge it the next time this professional demonstrates that they implemented what was discussed with them.

—Learning to give feedback has been an incredible growth experience for me —Lisa told me—. It is not enough to wait for an annual performance review to give feedback to my team members. Waiting that long can catch them off guard with unexpected areas for improvement, and they may have forgotten the event I am referring to in my conversation. In other cases, they may lose confidence in me as a leader for withholding information that would have helped them improve if they had implemented it immediately.

I recently worked with a renowned global pharmaceutical company to help establish a more fluid feedback culture. During my seminars, participants expressed they experienced anxiety when asking for feedback on their performance and even more so when giving feedback to others. We focused our time together in creating new habits. Want to know where we got started to create change? We took their bi-annual feedback events, which seemed too intimidating to them, and broke them down into smaller parts: micro-feedback sessions.

Instead of waiting for significant events to request or provide feedback, we planned to do so at least once a week, asking for specific feedback from their supervisors, peers, and other team members. The request had to be specific: «What do you think I did well, and what should I improve? Can you give me tangible examples? I am interested in knowing what you observed, as it will help me to grow.» Gradually, these professionals started demystifying these conversations, incorporating them more naturally into their schedules.

What challenges do you face when giving feedback to others? Do you think our cultural *simpatía* may be contributing to your discomfort? Can you implement mini-feedback sessions as a new routine, perhaps once a week? These sessions should not take more than 10 to 15 minutes, and their benefits can accelerate your professional progression and that of your team members.

As a manager, ask for feedback from your team members; when you receive it, thank them. Consider they may feel uncomfortable providing you with feedback. Receive it as an excellent gift for your growth, and if your feelings get a bit bruised in the process, remind yourself that feeling uncomfortable is only temporary, while that valuable information can have a long-term impact on your growth.

Pillar 3: Model the leadership style you would like to see in others

Being and modeling the change we want to see takes work. We are immersed in a system that generally lacks psychologically safe spaces where people can express themselves without fear of consequences. However, as managers and leaders, we can drive systemic change, starting with our teams. This may be the most challenging project we undertake because it involves a progressive shift in consciousness so that our teams operate under an abundance and collaboration mindset instead of from competition and scarcity. You may not see immediate results, encounter resistance, and be tempted to revert to operating as you were taught. Persisting on pivoting others' mindsets can be hard work, but it is necessary for humanity. Where to start? With you modeling for your team the qualities of that conscious and empathetic leader the world is crying out to see, qualities that you already possess.

A Forbes article mentions a study conducted in 2023 by Cynthia Adams, president of Leadership Circle. This study, which surveyed about 240,000 professionals, was vital in identifying the three main characteristics that make women more effective leaders than men.

First, women are more effective at building relationships that pursue the common good and are based on authenticity (exactly what younger generations prefer!). Female leaders focus on how far we could go together rather than maintaining an individualistic approach. Second, men tend to lead from a «play not to lose» mentality, focused on keeping at bay what they don't want to happen, while women tend to lead from a «play to win» perspective, focusing our energies on moving toward the vision of what is possible. These are two different approaches, and our reports usually notice the difference. Thirdly, women tend to cultivate deeper connections, as we often show genuine interest in others and get involved in mentoring them.

In the business world, these three areas constitute our superpowers. Don't let anyone convince you otherwise! Doing the work that needs to be done well is essential. If we also do it with a human-centered approach, we will create within our organization a robust community that many, especially young talent, will want to be part of.

Not all of us had the leaders we would have liked to have, but those experiences with a bad boss or a terrible client were not in vain. They happened so that you could be where you are today, with the opportunity to do it differently and create change in your space. Consider that to support others in reaching their full potential, we must see them succeed in our minds first. It will be very difficult to encourage them to grow if we hold a limited or flawed image of them in our minds. Dare to believe in others and imagine them in their best possible expression. This is your opportunity to start breaking the chain and to do what you would have liked others had done for you.

LESSONS LEARNED

- The transition from working as an individual contributor to becoming a team leader is perhaps the most important challenge of our professional lives. It invites us to develop new skills and confront limiting cultural messages about our role and capabilities as leaders.

- This stage offers you an opportunity to drive change. You can replicate the good things your previous bosses taught you and learn from past difficult situations to do it differently now that you are in charge.

- You will need to accept that there are people on your team with greater technical knowledge than you. You will shift from doing all the detailed work to directing and motivating your team towards a common goal without competing or proving that you know as much as them or more.

- In our Latin American culture, it has been historically rare to find women in leadership positions, which can make us feel intimidated in our leading role. In our collective unconscious, the role of Latina women has been to support others, not to lead spaces.

- Just as you seek to be aware of what motivates you to show up to work every day, it is equally important to understand what motivates your team members. This requires investing time with them and figuring out their deepest motivations.

- Providing feedback to team members can be quite uncomfortable due to our cultural *simpatía*, which leads us to maintain harmonious relationships and avoid potential conflicts.

- Giving frequent feedback is key to developing your team and gaining their trust as a leader. Giving feedback once a year deprives them of the opportunity to make immediate adjustments.

CHAPTER 11

Your career or your family?

On a gray and wintry morning in New York, my friend Melba, a Colombian immigrant and mother of two children born in the United States, let herself collapse on the icy bench that witnessed the thousands of tourists visiting the Brooklyn Bridge daily. The cold was relentless, penetrating through every tiny, invisible fiber of her clothes. With visible exhaustion and tears, Melba asked herself: «Whose life am I living?»

Mother, daughter, wife, sister, friend, coach, and much more, Melba was always willing to give her best to everyone. But this time, she felt very tired. Driven by exhaustion, she gathered the courage to ask herself: «How long will I keep living other people's lives? When will I start placing myself first without guilt?»

Although this story happened a few decades ago, Melba shared it with me just a few years back. Since then, the image of my friend sitting on that bench on a wintry day frequently haunts me. The cold, the loneliness, and the questioning whether I am living the life I chose or if I am letting the pressures around me dictate what my life should look like are all too familiar to me.

And you, whose life are you living?

PULLED IN MULTIPLE DIRECTIONS

Being a woman generally comes with the pressure of being pulled in multiple directions. At some point in our lives, we can find ourselves trapped in the impossible mission of giving our time, attention, and energy to the many opposing demands from family and work. And it's hard to choose. Culturally, family and friendships occupy a vital role in our lives. We come from a culture of sharing meals, events, and experiences in groups, of being together as a collective.

On the other hand, we are immersed in the Anglo-Saxon culture of hard work, productivity, and individualistic success. We operate in two worlds, and both demand such intensity that it can be challenging to keep up. Something has to give; generally, that is our health, rest, or enjoyment.

Many Latinas with whom I spoke feel the pressure, and sometimes the anxiety, that comes with having to balance so many balls up in the air. As trailblazers, we can feel misunderstood. We have the opportunity to create an impact in the world around us, one that our ancestors did not have the chance to develop, and we wonder where we will find the energy to take care of our loved ones and attend to family demands. So, we give in by putting ourselves last, taking care of our needs only if time and energy are left after attending to everyone else. In the meantime, our dilemmas and voices of guilt can frequently run through us: *I invested so much in my education that I want to succeed in my profession, but my family needs me, and I don't know if I can delegate those tasks to others. What do I do?; I stayed home for a while and felt guilty for not using my talents, so I went back out into the world to focus on my profession, and now feel guilty for neglecting my loved ones, or I have no choice but to check emails at night and on weekends, as I want my manager to know that I am committed to my career!*

Riddled by guilt and self-judgment, we try to cover all fronts by working harder at home and work. This not only happens to those of us who are mothers but also to those who are wives, partners, daughters taking care of elderly parents, or women who want to live a life that is more than just work. The pressure to place ourselves last is real, and in my experience as a mother and full-time professional, attempting to be it all for everybody can bring the most organized and disciplined among us to their knees.

I worked harder than everyone around me and placed myself last on my list of priorities because I wanted to feel like a good mother and a valuable professional. I slept little, ate almost nothing between breakfast and dinner, and worked until past midnight. I drugged my guilt and insecurities by checking work emails. These seem like small actions without severe short-term consequences, but their succession and accumulation culminated in my absolute collapse. So resounding that several years later I am still recovering.

According to McKinsey & Co., one in three women, or 60% of working mothers with young children, spend five or more hours daily on household chores and caring for loved ones. That is equivalent to a part-time job! Women not only face greater demands at home, but we also feel the pressure at work. The same report states that women support and mentor more colleagues and teams than men who hold similar jobs. We guide and mentor others to succeed in the workplace and are also 60% more likely to support our coworkers emotionally.

An equally interesting article from FastCompany indicates that women in executive positions are twice more likely than men to dedicate our time to diversity efforts. This is sometimes referred to as «office housework.» Beyond how ironic the term may sound, it resembles unpaid domestic chores, underestimated and not glamorous but essential! Women tend to shoulder these tasks more than men.

It will not surprise you then that millions of us have succumbed to work-related chronic exhaustion or burnout. Mayo Clinic defines burnout as a special type of work-related stress:

a physical or emotional exhaustion that involves a lack of sense of achievement and loss of personal identity.

An alarming 42% of women surveyed in 2022 feel burnt out, a significant difference compared to the 32% measured in 2021 and higher than the 35% reported by men. Younger generations report even higher rates of burnout, reaching an unsustainable 48% for ages 18 to 29. Our young people seek to live their lives beyond work, and they are wearing themselves out, pushing against a system that does not give room for that kind of life, mostly because those of us who came before paid our dues by working in sun and shade, and it is hard for us to conceive that the younger ones want to live in a more balanced way. It is hard to conceive that younger generations want to live a different life.

What hides behind our burnout? The ancestral, cultural, and often unconscious and implicit mandate that says that women must care for everyone around us. Being a good girl means we must attend to the needs of others, postponing any «selfish» attempt to prioritize our own needs. This is equivalent to an airplane pilot who abandons the cockpit amid an emergency to put oxygen masks on each passenger and crew member. Can you imagine? Remember what they say: put your oxygen mask first, then help others. I guarantee you that if you try to be everything to everyone, your plane will crash, affecting you and those around you.

DECISIONS THAT CHANGE THE COURSE OF OUR LIVES

—Of course, I'll be back. I'll be here in just a few months —I assured my boss, the marketing director for Airwick, the day we met behind closed doors in her office in Parsippany, New Jersey. My noticeable eight-month pregnant body announced my life would soon change—. I love my job, and I can't imagine not working.

«That's why I studied for so many years and sacrificed so much to live in the United States,» I thought.

At that very moment, as if letting me know that what I had just said was yet to be seen, my baby gave me one of those kicks that left me breathless. Just a few hours earlier, one of my colleagues and the father of two teenage children insisted that «something happens to moms the moment they hold their baby in their arms. Something changes in them.» How interesting. I wondered if this colleague and my unborn baby perceived something that I was not entirely seeing.

Two months later, holding a little Valentina, who was only a few weeks old, I glanced at my husband while trying to hold back my tears.

—What do you think? —he asked as we walked out of the third daycare center we had visited that day.

What to say? The smell of dirty diapers, babies crying while women in charge seemed overwhelmed, those neon lights on the ceiling, and not one Latina woman around. Those lovely strangers welcomed me with a smile while my eyes were fixed on their long and colorful nails, thinking, «How do they change a diaper without scratching the baby?» Postpartum really changes the way you think and see things.

—I can't do it! —I burst out, letting out a suppressed scream and crying my eyes out before Gonzalo, who was trying to understand what was happening. I felt my heart shatter in a thousand pieces. I couldn't leave my life's most important treasure for ten hours daily to return to my corporate career. Just thinking about that possibility was devastating. My work demanded that I be in the office five days a week with no chances of remote work; my husband worked at a bank more than an hour away from home and as many hours as I did, and our family was more than ten hours away by plane, I simply... couldn't. Leaving my 6-week-old daughter with strangers in a foreign country was much more complicated than I had imagined. I just couldn't. But how would we pay our bills? And the student loans we had accumulated with our MBAs? The financial impact of this decision would be significant for our family, but my entire being refused to return to the same corporate career into which I had invested so much and with which I had merged my identity and value. The detachment from that corporate identity would be brutal, and the process would continue for at least a decade, but I didn't know it at the time.

—I'll stay home with her for a few months, and then I'll figure out how to find a part-time job or something more flexible —I promised, tears rolling down my face and onto my daughter—. Keep focusing on your career; I'll stay with her for a few months —I proposed. Gonzalo nodded in silence. I don't think either of us really knew what we were doing. Isn't raising your children in a system that is not your own, whose values you have not yet made yours, and whose language you do not always understand a little bit of a life experiment?

Becoming a mother far away from your mother (and from your grandmother, aunts, and cousins) can have a profound impact on you. It had it on me. I don't know if I would have chosen it if I had the opportunity to shuffle my cards differently. But here I was, far away from every woman in my family, alone with my daughter in a small apartment all day and with tremendous guilt for leaving my professional life behind. The mental torture I imposed on myself was such that in less than a year, I was working again. After all, who was I if not a corporate professional? For years, that was the only vision of myself I held in my mind, merging my essence and personal value with my work and profession. I felt that without a profession, I was worth nothing. Not even the time with my beloved daughter could fill that inner void that I carried day and night, but I couldn't be separated from her either.

It was then that I decided to become a full-time mother and a full-time consultant for a medium-sized company, where they paid me part-time while I worked full-time hours. I accepted the money they offered me under the implicit promise that I would have some flexibility if my daughter got sick. So off I went, piloting a plane and constantly running up and down the aisle, putting oxygen masks on everyone except myself. As you already know, the plane of my life came crashing down a few years later.

DID I DO THE RIGHT THING?

I don't have enough pages in this book to tell you how many times I questioned if my decisions were correct. What would have happened if I had continued my corporate career in a multinational company instead of working as a consultant in a smaller company? Where would I be today, and how far would I have gone? Would I be more respected by those who don't open their doors for me today, no matter how persistently I knock on them? Would those work relationships be genuine, or would they be solely based on commercial interests? What would my relationship with my children be like if I had been absent most of the time because of work schedules and travel? Who am I now if I am no longer that corporate executive I thought I would be? Could I have done it differently? Did I do the right thing? Too many questions. No answers.

I can't really know where I would be today. And besides, what does «doing the right thing» really mean? The right thing for whom and according to whom? Is it the right thing for my life or somebody else's? When my mind starts to torture me, questioning a past that now, from a distance, looks so much easier, I go back to that moment when I held my daughter in my arms, and I know I did the best I could with the resources, support, and information I had. Part of my process of acceptance consisted of removing the implant of a corporate executive woman that I carried since my childhood and that I had merged with my life purpose and personal value. This process was about letting go of the corporate executive who was not, and that would never be, at least not how I had imagined her for decades. Some paths are simply not possible. If we don't allow ourselves the space to let go of our unfulfilled expectations and aspirations, we will continue to yearn to be that person who will never be, burdening ourselves with frustration and remorse.

Your story might be like mine, or perhaps it's quite the opposite. Perhaps your decisions were or would have been different, or maybe not. There is no perfect decision. There are simply unique and unrepeatable life paths.

GOING FOR IT ALL: YOUR CAREER AND YOUR FAMILY

To write this chapter, I connected with women I admire who did what was not possible for me: continue their full-time professional careers once they became mothers. I will share the insights and concrete strategies I extracted from these conversations so that you can apply the ones that may be most useful to you, whether you are a mother, plan to be a mother someday or care for other important people in your life.

I met Millie Guzmán four years ago when, after my burnout, I decided to explore the corporate space again. Millie is among the first women in her family to graduate from college and grow professionally. Despite pursuing a demanding career on Wall Street, where women are still underrepresented, Millie pursued her professional goals while being a mother, wife, and daughter involved with her family life.

—Tell me, how did you handle so many demands and pressures? —I asked her when we met—. How did you maintain your physical, mental, and emotional health, even your happiness, during the process?

Millie confessed that the first years were not easy.

—Adjusting from being a fast-paced career woman to becoming a mother was difficult. Something was not right. As the aunt of 18 nieces and nephews, I knew very well how to change and swaddle a baby, but when it came to doing it with my daughter, I felt anxiety and panic. I couldn't process that I had become the mother of another being, mainly because my daughter spent the first few days of her life in the neonatal unit. That meant fewer moments of contact with my baby, making it difficult to adjust to my new reality.

Millie also felt judged and surrounded by opinions about how she should or should not raise her daughter.

—Some people in our community can be very harsh with their opinions as if they had invented motherhood! —she told me, laughing. I went through the same thing: receiving instructions that not only felt intrusive to me but also made me feel useless.

A close friend realized Millie was having difficulty adapting to motherhood. Knowing that the gym had been essential to her social life before becoming a mom, she encouraged her to return. It was in that space Millie began to find her path to healing. That community of women where she felt heard and welcomed was vital to moving forward, as was her husband, her equal partner in the stage of being parents. That support group she could trust was fundamental in returning to work.

Even if we have remote and flexible jobs, support is equally important. Do you remember the video of a BBC interview with that man who, taking the videocall from his home, suddenly found his two daughters bursting into his office and his wife crawling on the floor, desperately trying to get them out of there? The video was hilarious and went viral in a short time. But if that happens to you as a woman, especially if it happens to you more than once, rest assured that your professional image will be affected. The same goes when children scream during our calls, or our elderly parents require our attention.

Any woman who works and has family responsibilities will tell you how life-saving a community is. What we don't talk about is that many of us find it challenging to delegate some tasks to others and place massive pressure on ourselves to do most of them alone. So, build your community and don't feel guilty about relying on it. Doing everything by yourself is possible but not sustainable.

DISTRIBUTE YOUR EMOTIONAL INVESTMENTS CONSCIOUSLY

—I made many adjustments to return to work. Being honest with myself, I realized that motherhood was not the only thing that defined me. It was just one of my dimensions.

For Millie, being a mother is a gift of life and the opportunity to love another being unconditionally. Even so, she wanted to continue being active in her multiple life dimensions.

—As a general practice, I always have a plan B to distribute my emotional investments. The key is to balance the different alternatives in which I can invest my time and energy. I didn't want to put everything into a single dimension because my heart called me to continue participating in other areas of my life. Also, returning to work was part of continuing to support my loved ones financially.

When Millie was at home, she was completely present with her family, and not with her mind lost in that problem that had been left unsolved or in those emails she hadn't managed to answer. And when she was at work, she focused on delivering excellence to continue earning the trust of others. Considering how our cultural tendency towards modesty can impact us, we must make ourselves more visible and active at work when our family demands increase. If you intend to continue growing in your professional life, this would be the least appropriate time to become invisible since you will be reinforcing a biased system that expects you to lower your level of participation at work when demands at home increase. Don't give them a reason to stop supporting your career!

The maternal penalty is defined as a series of barriers women face when becoming mothers that increase our income gap or delay the arrival of new growth opportunities. An article published in Business Insider mentions that 72% of mothers and fathers surveyed believe that women face additional barriers once they become mothers. Women are penalized because of the widespread expectation that we will be less committed to our work or distracted by the additional demands.

—I took small actions, such as gaining more visibility in some meetings, requesting to participate in new projects, and volunteering for certain opportunities. All these actions increased the credits building up in my professional credibility account —Millie told me—. I wanted others to know that I would continue to do impeccable work and that they could trust me. Then, when I needed it, I used some of those credits to leave work early when my daughter was sick or when she had events at her school.

Millie never apologized for being a mother. She never said, «I'm sorry, I must take care of my daughter.» How I wish I had heard this 15 years ago! Don't you find that we are often the ones who undermine our professional image by using disempowering language? I noticed men don't apologize in that way. To present ourselves confidently, we must be aware of how we express ourselves and of our words.

ACT OF HEALTHY REBELLION

Calculate how you divide your time today and how you would like to divide it from now on.

How would I redistribute my energy and time investments? What actions can I take to increase my professional

> *account credits, and how would I use them? Where can I delegate more?*
>
> _____
>
> _____
>
> _____
>
> _____
>
> **Develop your plan and start putting it into action.**

IS IT SELFISH TO ASK FOR WHAT YOU NEED?

Many of us are programmed to give but not to ask for what we need. How often do we anticipate receiving a *no*, so we do not even ask? How many other times do we want not to bother others, telling ourselves that they already have too much on their plate? This is like saying no to ourselves before we even verbalize our request. If we dismiss our needs, what do we expect others to do? They will probably put our needs in third or fourth place.

In our culture, where men ancestrally went out into the world to earn a living, and women stayed in charge of managing their homes and caring for their loved ones, the subconscious story we carry is that a woman who takes care of her home and family is fulfilling her obligations, while men who do so are going the extra mile and doing more than what is expected of them.

In Millie's words:

—When fathers say they need to leave early for their daughters' ballet recitals, they are exemplary parents. When we women say the same thing, we can be frowned upon. The standards are clearly different.

Take off the burden of feeling selfish. Stop telling yourself that you are a burden to others. Be aware of the very high standards you set for yourself while granting others the freedom to make mistakes. When will you grant yourself that same freedom?

ACCEPT THAT BALANCE DOES NOT EXIST!

Some time ago, during a webinar organized by a financial services company, a mother and professional panelist admitted that balance did not exist in her life. The rest of the panelists silently nodded their heads in agreement.
—Little things add up, and we find ourselves juggling —the panelist continued—. Sometimes, some of those things will inevitably fall to the floor.

ACT OF HEALTHY REBELLION

Review everything that happens in your life during a week and divide it into two columns: glass or plastic.

Which objects can't I drop? Which ones can I?

_____

_____

_____

_____

Be careful to include hours of sleep, nutrition, exercise, and emotional well-being in your list!

She provided an interesting illustration:
—Imagine that some of those things you juggle are made of glass, and others are made of plastic. The secret is to keep your eyes focused on the fragile ones, not letting them fall. Those are the ones you can't neglect.

CREATE YOUR ACTION PLAN

If something can bring us to our knees, it's not being able to keep up with the multiple responsibilities as our parents age and our children grow up.

Here comes a test because we've reached a critical moment in our journey. If you are like me, sometimes running from one thing to another as if on autopilot, you may resist answering the questions that come next. You may tell yourself that you will work on them on another day and with more time or that you want to get to the end of this chapter first. Rushing into what's next is a common habit for those of us who have a hard time placing ourselves first in our chaotic lives. Don't underestimate the importance of taking time for yourself, especially when your inner voice says, «Not now!» because that perfect moment may never come. This is your opportunity to do it differently.

ACT OF HEALTHY REBELLION

Reflect on the following questions:

What judgments against myself do I hold in my mind, and which do I decide to let go of today?

_____
_____
_____
_____

What internal dialogue would support me the most in this moment? What do I need to hear? What do I need to feel?

_____
_____
_____
_____

What areas of my life have I abandoned that I want to bring back?

_____
_____
_____
_____

> *Who is part of my support community,
> and how can they specifically help me?*
>
> _____
>
> _____
>
> _____
>
> _____
>
> _____
>
> *What adjustments do I want to make in my professional life
> to make my commitment and interest in my growth clear?*
>
> _____
>
> _____
>
> _____
>
> _____
>
> _____

ACCEPT YOU CAN'T HAVE IT ALL

Acceptance of what is, just as it presents itself, can be the first step towards our inner peace.

—Motherhood has been a path of constant acceptance for me. It wasn't always easy —Millie told me—. It was hard for me to accept that I probably was not going to be there when my daughter took her first step or spoke her first word. I had to admit that I wouldn't be present for everything.

I know this acceptance can be challenging and come loaded with guilt. It was for me. I had a hard time accepting that I would not be there when my daughter took her first step or spoke for the first time. And although I was there for those moments, today, more than a decade later, I don't remember many of them. In addition to not being able to trust a stranger to take care of my daughter Valentina, I had a deep fear of being judged as a bad mother if I left her with another person all day. I was overwhelmed thinking what people would say (¡Qué va a decir la gente!).

—In this process of acceptance, I didn't let guilt invade me or let the voices of self-punishment condemn me once again —Millie told me—. I repeated to myself that I was doing the best I could, that I was a good mother and that I was enough.

It was also crucial for Millie to accept that not everything would be possible in her professional life. When her daughter reached adolescence, Millie was offered a better job opportunity that would require many additional hours.

—I consciously decided to let it go —she told me, pausing—. Unfortunately, the opportunity presented itself at the most inconvenient moment, and I had to let that train go.

Like me, Millie asked herself several times what would have happened if she pursued that opportunity. With each question, she reminded herself that her decision had been thought through and that it was the best possible alternative for her daughter and her family.

—Given the circumstances, I made the best decision I could. That's not to say that the choice to be present for my family didn't impact my career trajectory —she added, as someone who has made peace with herself for that which was not feasible.

To find inner peace, we must practice compassion and self-forgiveness. It's not that you aren't capable, or that there's something wrong with you, or that you do everything wrong. It's that you are human and have limited energy and time. Accepting that not everything will be possible comes with some sadness and a bit of grieving. That's okay. Remember to treat yourself with dignity, forgive your judgments, and give yourself love and compassion, knowing you can only do what is humanly possible. Life is messy and imperfect; the sooner we accept this reality, the happier we will be.

LESSONS LEARNED

- Coming from a collectivist culture and immersed in the Anglo-Saxon culture of individualistic success, we live in two worlds with such intensity that something has to give. That is generally our health, rest, or enjoyment.

- 42% of women feel burnt out, compared to 35% of men. The percentage rises to an unsustainable 48% for young people aged 18 to 29.

- Behind our burnout hides the cultural mandate that says women must care for everyone around us. In our culture, being a good girl means attending to the demands of others while banishing any «selfish» attempt to prioritize our own needs.

- Some paths are simply not possible. If we do not allow ourselves the chance to let go of unmet expectations and aspirations, we will keep chasing the person we will no longer be, burdening ourselves with frustration and regrets.

- Any woman who works and has family responsibilities will tell you that community is a great salvation. However, many of us struggle to delegate and keep pressuring ourselves to do mostly everything alone.

- The message we carry in our subconscious is that any woman who takes care of her home and children is fulfilling the tasks assigned to her as a woman, while any man who does the same is doing more than what is expected of him.

- Running and running is a common pattern for those who find it hard to put ourselves first. Do not underestimate the importance of taking time for yourself, especially when your inner voice says, «Not now!» because the perfect moment may never come.

- Accepting that not everything will be possible comes with some sadness and a bit of grieving. That's okay. Remember to treat yourself with dignity, forgive your judgments, and give yourself love and compassion, knowing that you can only do what is humanly possible.

CHAPTER 12

Your future is not only in your hands

You will not achieve your professional goals alone. No matter how intelligent and hard-working you are, much of what our culture and our parents instilled in us regarding work will not be enough for you to advance in your profession.

Our culture pushed us to believe that someone would notice it and reward us if we put our heads down and worked hard. Nothing could be further from the truth. This concept may have helped our ancestors survive in factory and agricultural work environments where the goal was to achieve the most output in the shortest possible time. For many of them, there was no other option than to sacrifice a lot, or it all, to get their families ahead while not drawing much attention to themselves. We carry this concept of servile work rooted in our collective unconscious.

The opportunity before us looks like a relay race, where those who ran before our time only reached a certain level. They did the best they could. Now, we carry the baton and can go even further in our race, partly because of all that ancestral sacrifice. The race ahead invites us to come out of our isolation and the belief that we have to do it all by ourselves or that we don't deserve the time and support of others. Your success is as much an individual effort as a collective one.

Some time ago, I came across Harvey J. Coleman's success pie framework, or P.I.E. This acronym is a formula for understanding how we can grow professionally, and it collides with our ancestral way of thinking.

P stands for *performance* or how well we do the work assigned. According to Coleman, your performance represents only 10% of your success. You have to do your job well to grow in your profession, but that only accounts for 10% of the total. Therefore, putting your head down and doing an excellent job is not enough.

The letter *I* stands for *image*, which adds another 30% to your professional success. Your image includes your verbal and non-verbal communication, confidence in expressing yourself, ability to work in teams, and attitude when facing difficulties. What image have you been forging so far, and what changes can you introduce to be more effective? Look around you. Pay close attention to your company's leaders or clients if you are an entrepreneur. What do you observe? How do they present and conduct themselves, especially in challenging moments? What can you learn from those who have been successful in your professional space without losing your style or feeling that you need to change who you are?

The remaining 60% collides head on with our culture. The E that completes the acronym PIE is the most critical driver of our professional success and stands for *exposure* to key people. These are those who need to know about you and your work because they can support your growth. Much of your professional progression depends on them.

In my corporate career and later as an entrepreneur, I worked really hard but seemed to advance slowly. Although my image was strong and my attitude valued, that wasn't enough. Looking back, I realize I lacked the most essential pillar: a team of people committed to supporting my success. Culturally, we were not taught how to develop this key pillar. Now that we know this let's intentionally create the most critical asset for our professional advancement: our social capital.

Phyllis Barajas introduced me to this concept. She is a social entrepreneur and the founder and president of Conexión, a non-profit organization that supports Latino men and women in building their social capital. After working closely with Robert Putnam, a professor at Harvard University, author, and expert in social capital, Phyllis decided to help expand this concept in our community, aware of its transformative power. Phyllis' impact in our community has been such that she earned the nickname «Madrina,» which in our culture is reserved for those who have earned a special place in our lives and hearts.

Phyllis invited me to delve into Putnam's work, which defines social capital as «the connections between individuals, and the social networks and rules of reciprocity and trust that arise from them.» Putnam discusses connections between people and reciprocity in those relationships, meaning both parties must benefit. This mutual benefit is essential because some individuals can culturally operate from a scarcity mindset and tend to take more than what they give. He also mentions a mutual trust that develops over time, making these connections acquire real value. Those who understand how to create and utilize their social capital run with advantages: they identify and receive better professional opportunities, are more effective at work because of the doors opened for them, possess better stress management skills, and lead more satisfying lives.

Those of us who are the first in our families to access our professional spaces generally do not have those networks of connections and may be unclear on how to build them. Based on this, is our destiny influenced by our zip code?

CONNECTED FOR SUCCESS: BORN WITH IT, OR CAN YOU CREATE IT?

—Your zip code of birth can influence the trajectory of your professional career —said one of my interviewees—. Your friends and other social groups can influence your choices regarding pursuing a formal education, deciding where to study, or even what type of work to apply for.

There is some truth in *Tell me who you associate with, and I'll tell you who you are* since our environment has a significant influence on our actions, decisions, and results. However, having been born in a rural town far from any university or company that offered growth opportunities, I assure you with absolute confidence that your birth zip code does not define your path. There is some influence on your future journey, but nothing is set in stone. You are responsible for creating your path and building your social capital at every step. Don't let anyone put a limit on what you can achieve.

Andrew Rodriguez, a son of Ecuadorian immigrants, is the founder and president of a company focused on accelerating research and development in the biopharmaceutical industry. I met him at a Latino Leaders conference in Boston, and his demeanor during the event immediately caught my attention. Have you ever observed people's behavior at events? How many approach the speakers once they finish their panel or presentation? Very few. How many determinedly go around the event venue, connecting with new people instead of staying surrounded by their group of acquaintances? Very few. How many head without hesitation to people who hold higher positions or who have been notoriously successful? Very few.

We can feel intimidated by those who denote more authority or power than us. Andrew did the opposite. He did not stay in his seat but deliberately walked around the room to approach people of interest and introduced himself by shaking hands and giving them his business card. Andrew worked the event. And since I was doing the same, I approached him and gave him my card. We agreed to connect via Zoom when I returned to New Jersey.

When we connected, Andrew shared his experience in building his social capital. His turning point occurred when he arrived at Harvard for his Master's in Business (MBA) without knowing anyone and feeling out of place.

—I looked around, and it seemed everyone already knew each other. They came from similar schools and talked about companies I had never heard of —Andrew told me. Being a first generation in those elite spaces, Andrew did not yet have the social capital that many around him seemed to have—. As we are born into families without access to those networks of contacts, it is imperative that we intentionally create relationships and connect with other people, even when we feel that we are making an uncomfortable effort.

He confirmed that to create lasting relationships of mutual trust, one must learn to give and receive. It is not only about asking and taking. It must be reciprocal. During our virtual meeting, for example, Andrew was genuinely interested in learning about my journey and offered his support and network of contacts to help me advance my professional goals. But those words were not the end: after our Zoom meeting, he sent me a thank you email, and we agreed to connect again in a few months. In the meantime, he continued sending me links and information about my areas of interest.

During our conversation, I enjoyed learning that Andrew taught his children how to build their social capital early on.

—I serve on the board of directors of a non-profit organization that operates in the science and technology space —he told me—. I recently brought my 12-year-old daughter to one of their events. I wanted her to observe what happens in those spaces, learn how people connect, and interact with others herself.

This decision had such an impact that other board members opened some of the events for their children to participate in.

—We must stop asking for permission or wait for others to invite us —he told me. Putting an end to asking for permission or waiting to be invited is key, and it changed my life. Let's dare to step out of our comfort zones with determination and courage and show up in those spaces where we want to be.

In the last few years, building my social capital has accelerated exponentially. During most of my corporate career, I used to interact with the same small group of people, but when I launched my own business, I went out into the world to interact with hundreds of professionals in a very short time. As the introvert that I am, that was very challenging. I had to overcome my inner voice: *What if I go to that event and don't know anyone? How would I look standing in a corner watching others engaged in their conversations? How do I make it sound like I'm not trying to sell them something?*

I attended my first big event with a friend who, like me, did not have much experience in those situations. We stayed close to the food and drinks as we noticed more traffic there. We were hoping to meet someone interesting, and we were right, as I left with several new connections. Later on, I showed up to many other events by myself and without knowing anyone, something that in the recent past would have seemed like a crazy thing for me to do. Initially, it was uncomfortable, but I didn't allow my inner voices to hold me back. I approached new people and showed curiosity about their profession or business, just like Andrew did. I led by listening, connecting, and not trying to sell them anything, even when I knew my business would greatly benefit from that potential income. I learned that trying to sell in an initial conversation was like proposing marriage on the first date. We don't do that! Genuine and valuable relationships are built with time and patience.

In only four years, I went from knowing a few dozen people to connecting with several hundred, all by showing up in spaces where I didn't know anyone. Today, when I visit a given city in the United States, I know I will have at least one or more connections with whom to have a coffee or lunch since I took the time to build those relationships, driven by my need to connect with people and feel part of my community. Sales came almost organically later, and I also gained new friends who enriched my life. Attending events can offer outstanding learning experiences. I noticed that those who step out of their professional space to go to events and conferences and make themselves more visible and valuable in our community can transform the perception of their professional brand, building credibility in their workplace and with their leaders and attracting better opportunities. Therefore, don't just stay working in front of your laptop: go out into the world to make yourself known and build your brand and social capital.

TAKE THE PRESSURE OFF DURING NETWORKING

I led a seminar on this topic some time ago and asked the audience to raise their hands if networking came naturally. Less than 10% of the room did. Several confessed that the word networking made them anxious because it sounds like something too transactional when we are culturally wired to build natural and genuine connections with others. Networking can feel forced, and even the thought that we must sell something to others causes us to resist doing it.

Let's pivot this concept in your mind so that you can build your social capital more fluidly.

What if you give a new meaning to the word networking, changing it from «connecting with others to obtain a commercial advantage in return» to «creating a relationship with another human being in which both potentially support each other in the future?»

You don't have to sell anything to anyone on that first encounter. Take that pressure off your shoulders. Nor do you have to seek their approval or force them to understand what you do if the conversation does not want to go there. Building valuable relationships is not about the words you speak to others but about how you make them feel. Let go and be yourself, flow, have fun, and do it as we do in our Latino culture, without rigidity or pre-existing formulas. Connect and express yourself from that deeper place of your essence, not just with a prefabricated phrase that describes what you do and has been rehearsed a thousand times. You come from a culture of relationships and genuine interest in others. Create a good experience for both of you. You carry it in your DNA!

Phyllis explained how Robert Putnam studied two types of social networks we should build. In my experience, we tend to focus on one as the other feels outside our comfort zone.

On the one hand, we have bonding social networks. In our case, this network would be built with other Latinos and Latinas, particularly those with whom we feel validation and affirmation because we have much in common, such as country of origin, language, or race. Humans naturally tend to gravitate towards others we can relate to. However, the sense of belonging ignited by these networks can limit the expansion of our social capital. When I first arrived in the United States, I only wanted to surround myself with other Spanish-speaking Latinos. I observed something similar in Latina entrepreneurs who surround themselves mostly with others with similar profiles or in corporate employees who are limited to networking with similar people, event after event. Can you imagine the opportunities that could arise if these groups interacted with others more often? That's why bonding networks are necessary, but they are insufficient.

On the other hand, there are bridging social networks. These networks bring together people from different backgrounds and environments. While these individuals seem to have little in common, their association is instrumental in breaking down systemic barriers. In other words, if we want to break the glass ceiling and continue growing, the most effective way is to create trusting relationships with different people. These relationships will be based on mutual listening and learning from each other.

—We need both types of networks —Phyllis said—. Both the network of people who are similar to us and the network of people who are different and will help us enter spaces where we are currently absent. And since classism still wreaks havoc of division and separation in the Latino community, we must develop those bridging networks even within our community, uniting and supporting each other regardless of social class.

I couldn't agree with Phyllis more. A significant percentage of Latinos come from working-class families, and a minority come from spaces with connections and intergenerational knowledge of building their social capital. We must intentionally transfer this knowledge to those who do not yet possess it.

However, not everyone is willing to share their contacts and knowledge on how to build their social capital with other Latinos. I experienced it firsthand. I knocked on hundreds of doors, one after the other, and many never opened. Some of those people took the stage and microphones, talking about their mission to support our Latino community, yet when I knocked on those doors, there was no response. And when there was, they recommended that I buy a book to learn how things are done or hire a coach to help me. When people with power take up spaces to boast about what in reality they don't do, they hurt our community. I'm sharing this not as a judgment to those individuals but so that you are prepared when you knock on those doors that seem accessible but are not. If that happens, shake off the sour taste of rejection and keep trying elsewhere, accepting that not everyone will be for you.

I found it's been easier to break down classist barriers with non-Latino individuals than with people from our community. Many outside our community are willing to help us, so I suggest you list people you would like to connect with, particularly those with whom you feel a little uncomfortable but know can bring great value to your life. If you struggle like I did with asking for help or fearing bothering others, it may not be easy, but the effort will be worth it.

EXPAND YOUR NETWORK OF MENTORS

In your professional journey, you will find two types of people who can open both your mind and the doors of opportunity: your mentors and your sponsors. Each one has a unique role.

A mentor can guide you on technical issues and provide emotional or psychological support based on their knowledge and experience. They are like trusted advisors who help you challenge your thinking and belief system and help you see what you may not see clearly, whether due to lack of experience or because you are too close to the situation or problem. A sponsor has a different role: they use their social capital and put their name and reputation on the line to help you grow.

ACT OF HEALTHY REBELLION

Make a list of potential mentors. Choose people with different levels of experience, from different cultures, and with different worldviews. Write them down below:

_____

_____

_____

_____

Each person can give you their perspective based on their own experiences, so it is in your best interest to listen to as many viewpoints as possible and then make the decision that best aligns with your goals.

Those who know the value of mentorship understand the power of having several mentors and know that intentionally structuring a board of advisors is better than having a random group of mentors. That board is a group of diverse and consciously chosen people you can consult frequently. As with any board, you will want a variety of experiences, industries, genders, races, and ages.

Some time ago, I met for breakfast with Lucy, a partner at one of the largest consulting firms in the world, to discuss this topic. Born in Puerto Rico, she was the first in her family to attend college at Harvard University. Within a few months of arriving in Boston, she began to build her network of mentors in the most unexpected way.

—When I arrived at Harvard, I was super intimidated, and every time I passed the statue of John Harvard in the center of Harvard Yard, I would say: «Please help me survive another semester.» It was a significant change for me —Lucy confessed.

During her first year, her chemistry professor was a renowned Nobel Prize laureate.

—He was a warm and human person. A normal person. He told us that he would be in the cafeteria once a week and that we could sit down and talk to him. I was one of the few who did it. Surprisingly, very few people took the opportunity to talk to a Nobel laureate who wanted to offer us mentorship. Imagine the confidence that gave me and all I learned from him.

That was just the beginning of a series of valuable relationships in Lucy's professional life. That first experience helped her feel deserving of receiving support from those in spaces she aspired to reach. Feeling deserving instead of guilty and trusting that we have much to contribute to others is vital to expanding our networks.

—We Latinos tend to see ourselves as very social beings, but sometimes, we are only social in environments we know. That's why our network of professional contacts tends to be small, which is a dichotomy —Lucy told me—. I have seen how other ethnic and racial groups have much more sophisticated networks than ours. Therefore, the opportunity we have ahead of us is significant.

Here's proof that our culture gave us tools to build relationships, but we have not been using them to their fullest extent, possibly due to limiting beliefs.

Lucy transformed casual office relationships into mentoring opportunities, which eventually turned into sponsorship. Leaders who initially provided her guidance supported her in obtaining her next promotion or an important assignment. It all started with saying «Good morning» to those who occupied neighboring offices, followed by engaging in a dialogue about what projects each one was working on, and continued with Lucy being summoned by project leaders to work in their teams. It all evolved organically. For this process to take place in your life, you need to be aware of your internal dialogue when going after those mentors and how you hold yourself back.

WHERE DO I START?

I don't want to be a bother. He's so busy; What will they think if I ask for help? Will they see me as incapable of doing it alone?; What if he says no?; How do I ask for what I need?; What if it ends up being weird and I don't know how to break the ice? If we don't have the social capital others have built, we may be limiting ourselves by giving space to inner voices of fear and unworthiness.

Asking for help is still the hardest thing for me. I learned from my parents to be mindful about not being a bother to others, something I still hear from them every time they visit. They must have heard it during childhood when children were not allowed to participate in conversations with adults. When I ask for help, I acknowledge that I am vulnerable and I don't have all the answers, something that still makes me uncomfortable. It's like breaking down the image of perfectionism I carefully built over decades.

As the first in my family to go to college and enter in corporate spaces, I learned to figure things out independently because I felt there was no other option. I just had to keep moving forward. I had no alternative; I couldn't fail; too much was at stake. Those days I stopped for a minute and looked around to see who I could ask for help with that math problem, for instance, I couldn't find anyone. Ask the teacher for help? Never. I had to show her that I knew everything. Later, I would drag that thinking into my adult life. Collecting battles fought alone and in silence, I proudly proclaimed, «I did it! And I did it all by myself!»

There comes a time when the flag of *doing it all alone* that we wave with pride becomes a limitation. Our drive and pride brought us to where we are, but it is also true that if we want to play in the big leagues, we must do it differently. We have to do it as a team.

Let's embark together on a great act of rebellion: end the story that says we are a bother, not worthy of help, or better to manage on our own. No more pretending that we know what we are doing all the time. We need the help of others. There's no way around it. Believing that this help is available and that you deserve to receive it is part of an abundance mentality, and believing that this help is not available to you is a thought that comes from scarcity. Where would you say you are today?

For those born in the United States to immigrant parents, who became translators of the language and the system, an additional barrier may arise: the resistance to ask for help from people with authority or power. We are no longer talking about feeling like a bother; we are talking about the real consequences of trauma inflicted on millions of Latino children by authority figures. These experiences left a deep mark on our community. Those who during their childhood were diminished or felt discarded by people who in some way represented the system may experience resistance or anger when asking for help in their adult life, especially when asking for help from people in spaces of power. If this is your case, here is your opportunity to begin your healing journey and forgive those who inflicted pain on you by abusing their space of power or by making you feel ashamed for being Latina, for coming from an immigrant family, or for living in poverty. Do not allow these people to remain present, robbing you of the opportunity to receive support from those who genuinely wish to help you. Let go of that past with forgiveness and compassion. Remember that the only way to get ahead is together and not divided.

Not many of us dare to build our network of mentors. An article published by Neal, Boatman, and Miller indicates that 63% of women never had a formal mentor, even when more than half of their organizations have a formal mentor system. A Gallup report mentioned by El Puente Institute in a recent article shows a similar story for Latinos, highlighting that 60% of us do not have a mentor. We might not be fully leveraging existing opportunities and resources, either because we are unaware of them or hesitant to take action. Something similar happens to business owners.

This lack of mentoring is not only a reflection of our inaction as women, but also hint that some men have begun to be reluctant to meeting with women. According to a 2019 survey by Lean In, 60% of men in managerial positions feel uncomfortable participating in work-related activities involving women, such as providing mentoring, working alone with another woman, or socializing. That percentage was only 46% the year before. Numbers look more alarming among the executives surveyed, as they are 12 times more reluctant to meet alone with a woman in their workspace than with a man; when it comes to business travel, they are 9 nine times more hesitant to travel with women than with men, and for business dinners, six times more reluctant.

These statistics reflect a real fear among men, as misunderstandings could put their careers at stake. This creates a significant disadvantage for women, but once again, you have the power to create change. A good strategy is to be specific when requesting time with a leader inside or outside your organization. Introduce yourself and state your intentions: «I admire who you are as a leader, and I would appreciate your guidance and advice for my career. Would you have twenty to thirty minutes to meet?» Ask for help without hesitation, and clearly explain what you seek to obtain from the meeting. The more clarity you provide, the greater the likelihood that your request for time will be accepted.

In this chapter, Phyllis helped us understand how crucial it is to build our social capital. Andrew taught us to expand it through giving before receiving. Lucy inspired us to sit in front of those who seem unreachable, trusting that we have much to offer and relying on our cultural power to build genuine relationships. Let's not wait any longer. If we want to change the system, it is up to us to approach others who can support us in our journey, and if the pieces of the puzzle fall into place and the relationship prospers, we can, over time, convert them into our most faithful mentors, advocates, and sponsors.

LESSONS LEARNED

- You will not achieve your professional goals alone. No matter how intelligent and hardworking you are, much of what our culture and our parents instilled in us about work will not be enough for you to advance in your profession.

- To grow in your profession, you have to do your work and do it well, but the quality of your work represents only 10% of what will define your professional success.

- 60% of your professional success depends on your exposure to key people who need to know you and learn more about your work to support your path.

- Looking back, I realize I had missed the most crucial pillar: a team of people supporting my success. Culturally, we have not been taught how to build our social capital.

- Since many of us were born into families without access to those networks of contacts, it is important for us to pave our own way, creating relationships and intentionally connecting with other people, even if it feels uncomfortable.

- We need to stop asking for permission or waiting to be invited. We must dare to step out of our comfort zone with determination and courage to present ourselves in the spaces where we want to be.

- What if you give a new meaning to the word networking, changing it from «connecting with others to gain a commercial advantage» to «creating a relationship with another human being in which both potentially support each other in the future»?

- You don't have to sell anything to anyone in a first encounter. Remove that pressure. You also don't have to seek their approval or try to have them understand what you do if the conversation is not going there. Building valuable relationships is not about what you tell them but how you make them feel.

- A mentor is someone who can offer you guidance on technical issues and emotional or psychological support based on their knowledge and experience. A sponsor uses their social capital and puts their name and reputation on the line to help you grow.

- Our culture has provided us with tools to build relationships with others, but we have not used them in our professional spaces, possibly due to limiting mindsets.

- There comes a time when the pioneer flag we proudly wave because we achieved so much by ourselves can become a limitation. Our drive indeed brought us to where we are, but it is also true that we need to do it differently from now on. We need to do it as a team.

CHAPTER 13

Sponsors: Our missing link

The most important relationship in your professional life will be with a sponsor, and ironically, it can be the most difficult for us to create.

«No one makes it alone. The most important decisions about your career, such as promotions, salary adjustments, and the projects assigned to you, are discussed behind a closed door and in a room where you will not be present,» says Carla Harris, an African American executive, author of three books, and speaker.

Something similar happens with business owners. The decisions to grant you a contract are not made with you sitting at the table but behind closed doors among those with the decision-making power. Therefore, those of us who own our businesses also need those sponsors.

For most Latina women, sponsorship is a missing link in our professional lives, becoming one of the main reasons we do not advance as others. A 2022 Gallup research confirms that 40% of Latinos and Hispanics have a mentor, and only 21% have a sponsor. This small percentage is also the lowest of all demographic groups. We are behind even on this front, but the keys to starting to create these relationships are in our hands. Once again, we have the power to create our future.

—I turned to someone who had a seat at the table and could support my career —says Carla in an article published by Chief, explaining how she asked one of her mentors to sponsor her—. I mentioned that it was vital for me to get a promotion that year. There was nothing more I could say or show the organization to demonstrate I was ready or deserving. I told him, «You and I know the importance of having a person at the table who supports you. You know me, you know my work, you know the positive opinion of our clients. I believe you are the perfect person to support my career in that room.» —Carla was direct and received a yes from that individual. That conversation was crucial for her since if the person said no, they would have to explain why, and that information would be precious to Carla. But since they said yes, Carla trusted she would be well represented. However, she didn't stop there—. Since I'm inclined to keep insurance and since I knew another influential person who would be in that room, I also asked that second leader for support. So, if my first sponsor happened to feel weak when it came to fighting for my case, there would be a second voice of support.

This direct style is standard among white, non-Latino men in competitive sectors such as finance. Those who are afraid to ask directly are left behind in those spaces. This style can generally be more difficult for women because, at some point, we were told that we asked for too much, that we were bossy or demanding, or we may have been shamed in front of others when we were direct and assertive. Carla and many women I admire for their confidence and strength naturally handle this style, which works for them. I wonder what path they traveled before making their bold asks.

YOUR SPONSOR: AN ADVOCATE IN FRONT OF THOSE WHO DECIDE

A sponsor advocates for you, putting their name and credibility on the line to support your cause and to use their carefully built social capital for your benefit. The sponsor takes a risk:

his credibility will be at stake until your work and its results prove your worth to the group he endorsed you to. A sponsor can operate behind closed doors, such as when talking about promotions, opportunities, or salaries, or they can do it in front of you, such as when they amplify your work in public, give you exposure to the leaders of your organization, or invite you to events where they connect you with key people.

Consider your sponsor as an agent of your brand. Unlike a mentoring relationship, where the relationship is developed exclusively between the giver and the receiver, a sponsorship relationship incorporates a third group: the public before whom your brand must be promoted. Your sponsor's role will be to influence and direct this audience to support your professional goals. Remember when we talked earlier about the importance of creating your professional brand? A sponsor will elevate your game to a completely different level: you will no longer be the only one communicating the value of your brand; you will now have a highly credible representative with their social capital as an asset to amplify your visibility. You will be playing in the big leagues.

Sometimes, your sponsor will be somebody who is initially your mentor supporting you with their guidance and who later on decides to embrace your cause and advocate for you. In other cases, they may not have been a previous mentor. Some of the Latina women I interviewed had African American men and women or members of the LGBTQIA+ community as their sponsors. In recent years, both these communities found their voice and advanced their professional paths. Some other Latina women found their sponsors in non-Latino white men and women, who are generally more present in spaces of influence and power.

Stay open because your sponsor may come from the most unexpected place, and at the same time, stay alert for signs that indicate that a sponsorship is possible. I will discuss that next.

WHAT LEADS SOMEONE TO DECIDE TO SPONSOR ANOTHER PERSON?

Given the notorious lack of sponsorship for Latino professionals, I started to ask myself: what makes a person decide to sponsor another professional? What characteristics and values are repeated from sponsor to sponsor? What do sponsors think? Why do they choose to help others?

A conversation I had with Santi Strasser was revealing in that sense. Santi came to the United States from Argentina at 18, and since then, his professional career and social capital have experienced exponential growth. Santi co-founded Carbe Diem, an innovation and entrepreneurship platform within the prestigious consumer goods company General Mills. Santi could not have achieved his success without having learned to network with other people and without sponsors who opened doors for him. In the process, he paid attention to what makes a sponsor support us.

—As soon as I arrived in the United States without knowing anyone, I became aware of the importance of connecting with new people —Santi said. Through trial and error and trying again, as entrepreneurs do, Santi noticed certain patterns and habits in his sponsors that coincide with what I identified in the dozens of interviews I conducted.

—Those who sponsor others are givers who find a purpose in helping —Santi explained. Those who sponsor others from different environments, races, or ethnicities are moved by a deep sense of giving rooted in doing something good for others, seeking social justice, or correcting inequalities. Sponsors generally have an abundant mindset. They do not just stay focused on their business or career but broaden their scope to include the success of others.

—In many cases, sponsors see something of themselves reflected in you, like an earlier or younger version of themselves. In other cases, they see in you something that they want to support and leave as their legacy to the organization or the community —Santi added.

I want to compare a sponsor with someone who invests money, accepting a risk in exchange for a return. For the sponsorship of others to continue, the person who puts their social capital and name at risk must receive a return or benefit. This return can come in several forms, such as satisfaction for doing something good for another person or group (emotional benefit), an increase in the sponsor's credibility once the sponsored person is successful, making the sponsor look very good (benefit for the sponsor's professional brand), or an expansion of the sponsor's connections when the sponsored is successful and, in turn, opens valuable doors for the sponsor (social capital benefit).

ACT OF HEALTHY REBELLION

Reflect on your current and potential sponsors. Answer:

What benefit do I think they seek to obtain by deciding to support me?

_____

_____

_____

_____

It's important that you identify this benefit because, through your actions, you can help your sponsor achieve it in the same way Santi ensures his investors see a return on investment when they give him money to grow Carbe Diem.

HOW TO EARN A SPONSOR

Cover the basics: do your job and make yourself known

As my friend Dr. Gail Ayala Taylor says, «Mentoring is given, sponsorship is earned.» What does she mean by this? At a minimum, you must «meet certain requirements» that earn your sponsor's trust. Perhaps the most important requirement is your ability to do your job and do it well.

Let's continue with Lucy, whom I introduced in previous pages. When I asked her if she had to explicitly ask for sponsorship, she said it wasn't necessary. Much of her professional success was dedicating herself to doing her job excellently. This demonstrates the need to show the value of our work before a potential sponsor takes risks for us.

In her early years working at the consulting firm, Lucy took the time to converse briefly with her colleagues and superiors when she arrived at the office and chatted about their projects and clients. Over time, these informal talks put her on the radar with certain partners until one of them invited her to participate in a proposal he was putting together. Lucy said yes without hesitation. She had the time to take that project on and felt that doing so would open up career opportunities for her. Her intuition was correct. Through this project, the partner witnessed Lucy's values and abilities, after which he recommended she work with other partners in the firm. In a short time, Lucy had four different sponsors, all Indian.

—While I never asked them to sponsor me in meetings where promotions were decided, I am convinced that I am now a partner because of their support and influence —she said—. They opened doors for me and placed me on visible teams from which I could create valuable relationships with other members of the firm and with clients. That support resulted from the energy and time I invested in making myself known and showing interest in their projects.

Never underestimate the power of a seemingly small action when building new relationships. As we discussed, accumulating small actions outside our comfort zone can produce exponential results to advance our careers. Lucy's story is a true testament that the uncomfortable is worth it.

Dare to knock on the doors of the powerful

As you grow, you start to interact more with people in positions of power and leadership who will, in one way or another, be involved in your professional journey. Don't wait too long to connect with them because the sooner you understand their thoughts and the faster they have you on their radar, the better.

I met Carolina Alarco at a Latino Leaders event. Born in Peru, the founder of Bio Strategy Advisors and an investor in the biotechnology industry caught my attention because she built relationships with other professionals in spaces of power, something that many Latina women shy away from. Unlike what happens to Carolina, we tend to hold ourselves back with thoughts like *Meet with that older white man? No way. It's going to be too uncomfortable. We are too different.* We can become experts at finding differences without realizing that, in doing so, we create separation from others. If we focus on how uncomfortable we may feel, we lose focus on the goal of these relationships: build bridges, learn from others, and make our good work and contributions to the company's success known.

Carolina broke through those conditioning factors and intentionally created relationships that led to mentoring first and then sponsorship.

—I started asking executives for time when I was about 28 years old and held a managerial position —she told me—. Since I had been working hard at that company for a few years, I created a reputation for doing my job well, which helped a lot to open those doors.

Carolina prioritized connecting with people who could provide her with information she could apply to her job.

—I started connecting with older people, mostly white men I respected. Back then, most of the high-level executives in biotechnology were white men, excellent professionals who greatly supported my career. I would request lunch with one of them once a month, organizing directly with their secretaries and being very clear about the purpose of the meeting: I wanted to ask for their advice and guidance on issues related to my work.

With this strategy, Carolina had 30 to 45-minute monthly lunches with two or three executives from the company. She would meet with each one of them once per quarter, except with those who were very busy: with them, she would meet once a year. Every time they left the company building to walk to the nearest restaurant, these leaders would thank her, saying, «This is great! I needed to get out of the office.»

Before these meetings, Carolina prepared interesting questions about industry trends and the business. She thought in advance about what advice she would ask regarding situations she was going through in her day-to-day work. As the relationship evolved, she also provided feedback about interesting presentations they had made that Carolina had liked.

—My meetings were all business. I did not touch on personal topics where there could be drama, like family, children, or health. I learned that scared them away —she confessed—. If they ask you how your children are doing, making a short, positive comment is okay. It worked for me to keep these relationships on a strictly professional level. As Latinas, we need to be careful not to offer too much information or sound like we are complaining, as we tend to do within our community. Cultural differences can work against us.

To prepare for these conversations, pay attention to the language of the leaders of your organization or client. They can be formal and direct and not get into the details of the conversation as we would in other spaces. You may have to articulate your ideas or questions in fewer words and get to the point. Beyond the specific words you use, own your space and project your voice with confidence. Remember that you deserve to be there and deserve their support and guidance.

During our chat, Carolina shared how she ensures there will be a subsequent meeting. Unlike what many suggest, Carolina does not send a thank-you email but instead thanks them towards the end of the meeting and takes the opportunity to ask, «Do you think we could meet again in a few months? I want to continue this conversation.» The answer is usually yes. Then she contacts their secretary again to place the next meeting on the calendar.

When they get to know each other, and after about two or three meetings, she tells them: «I greatly value your guidance and what you do for me. I consider you my mentor.» Carolina does not ask these leaders if they want to give her mentorship but rather declares it. If we ask for mentorship too formally, especially when these leaders still don't know us very well, we might scare them as they might think: «I'm going to have to spend all these hours with this woman.» I know it because I experienced it firsthand!

Some time ago, I approached a Latina woman who had given a talk about mentorship and sponsorship at a conference, sharing a formula on how to approach a potential mentor or sponsor. Following the steps of her formula, I requested her mentorship, and she literally freaked out. That day, I learned that even if we follow the rules that seem to work for someone else and make our ask in the way they want to be asked, someone who doesn't know us may not feel ready for the commitment that a mentorship relationship implies.

Therefore, rather than focusing on what we need or will ask from them, it is better to create an experience where potential mentors or sponsors feel valued and not demanded or obligated.

Similar to what happened with Lucy, Carolina told me that she didn't ask any of these leaders to sponsor her, although some became sponsors on their own initiative. When promotion opportunities arose, her sponsor said, «Carolina is excellent. She will do a great job in that position. She is detail-oriented, serious, focused on execution, and knows her job.» They recommended her without her having to ask for it.

—Most interestingly, the relationship changed over time, and they asked me for advice regarding specific company strategies. They respected my point of view to the extent that after some time, they invited me to the company's strategic meetings, and that's how I started to participate in the decision-making process —Carolina told me. They began to see her as their peer.

Help your sponsor do their job

Carla Dodds, born in Argentina and raised in Texas, was an executive at Walmart and Mastercard before launching her independent consulting business. She called me to update me on her job search some time ago. She had decided to return to a corporate career and was knocking on the doors of people who knew her well to find those who could be her sponsors.

—I just finished a call with a person who could be my sponsor for an exciting opportunity —Carla told me—, and I had an epiphany.

I listened carefully. Knowing Carla, her epiphany would also be of great value to me.

—I realized that many people are willing to help but don't know how. So, while they could open doors for us as sponsors, they limit themselves to providing guidance and advice as a mentor would. We end up with a large number of mentors and no sponsors.

In other words, we end up with a lot of advice on how to do things, but few open doors for our progress and professional growth. If you can relate to this situation, consider taking a step back to ask strictly for what you need. When things don't seem to move on their own, it's up to us to take action, either by explicitly asking for a connection with another professional, by offering our name for a specific position, or by sharing our resume with influential people, in some cases, giving them in writing the words we want them to use to introduce us and open those doors.

Carla left me with a fundamental lesson that day. We must be clear about what we want and why and articulate it into a specific request. If we don't, we may miss opportunities.

And beyond the words you choose to express your request, remember that what's important is the trust you convey.

To understand how to increase our chances of gaining a sponsor, there's nothing better than asking them what makes them want to sponsor others. As part of writing this book, I asked several of them: «What do you need to see in someone to want to sponsor them? What do they have to do to make your job as a sponsor easier?» In other words, what do we need to do, as sponsorship seekers, to create a positive experience for our sponsors?

The answers were varied. In addition to trusting that we can do our work with excellence, sponsors value having clarity on our interests and goals so they can negotiate on our behalf. During a negotiation, information is power, so we need to be transparent with our sponsors and provide them with relevant information. I like to share with them my achievements and interests, the barriers and obstacles I face, and my vision of where I would like to take my professional life. I learned that transparency and vulnerability are part of creating that experience that will keep sponsors wanting to champion my brand.

FOR ENTREPRENEURS, SPONSORS ARE KEY

Most of us know the importance of having a sponsor if we are employees of a corporation or organization. But what about entrepreneurs? Even more so! Sponsors are key to the success of small business owners. They can use their social capital to recommend our work, give us visibility on important platforms, or help us grow our sales.

Recently, my business was blessed with a sponsorship that came most unexpectedly. It was all a succession of what looked like coincidences. Life blessed me twice, as I cannot tell if the sponsorship happened before the friendship or if it was the other way around. Everything seemed to happen simultaneously, shattering my beliefs that friendship and business cannot mix.

This story began a couple of years ago when I was conducting free seminars to expand my brand, those that make you wonder if they will ever lead to something. In one of those virtual seminars, I gave my online course away to attendees to encourage their participation. The winner was Lory Burgos, Marketing Director at a renowned insurance company. She later confessed that she wasn't sure why she had decided to connect to the seminar, as she usually didn't participate in those events. Thanks to that invisible hand that guides our destiny, I connected with Lory, who came to understand my work in depth and then hired me to run a series of seminars on the Latina Style platform.

Latina Style is an organization that, for more than thirty years, has recognized the work of thousands of Latinas in corporate spaces, entrepreneurship, and the armed forces and that facilitates access to knowledge and connections through its seminars and events. During the four seminars Lory invited me to conduct, I met Lupita Colmenero and Robert Bard, the chief operating officer and chief executive officer of Latina Style, respectively.

Val, would you share today's slides with me? Lupita asked after my third seminar, during which we identified our limiting cultural mindsets.

—Of course! —I said. I didn't usually share my slides after seminars, but something called me to do it. A few days later, I connected with Lupita over the phone to get to know each other better, and a few months later, I was on Zoom with her and her husband, Robert. In those conversations, we shared our stories and experiences and began to explore ways to collaborate.

—Val, why don't you bring your book to the Diversity Conference we are organizing in Washington, DC? —Lupita and Robert offered. It had only been a few months since I had launched *Uncolonized Latinas*, a book that Lupita had read and found very valuable. That conference would offer significant visibility for my work since they would award top leading Latinas in corporate and best Latino ERGs (employee resource groups). It was the ideal space to bring my work to hundreds of professionals who could benefit from it.

Lupita and Robert not only opened doors for me to bring my book to their conference, allowing me to place it in the hands of the most powerful Latinas in the country, but they also set up a massive table with my books at the most strategic and highly trafficked point in the room. There was a before and an after for my brand with Lory's sponsorship and this generous action from Lupita and Robert. My social capital and credibility increased significantly, and the contacts, additional sponsors, and friendships that emerged from that event were as valuable as they were unexpected.

It would be transformative for our community if more of these sponsors existed for Latina women, particularly within corporations awarding contracts to Latina entrepreneurs. We face such significant barriers for our businesses that sponsors within those corporations could make our work's value known internally and help us overcome bureaucratic obstacles so that we can be granted one contract opportunity to demonstrate what we are capable of doing. We still have plenty of magic left to create.

Let go of the belief that you may be a bother to others or that you don't deserve the help of those who hold the keys to your growth in their hands. Out in the world, there are thousands and thousands of people whose purpose is to help others. You can become the channel that allows them to do good. A considerable change in mindset is required in our community: to pivot from feeling like a charity project to becoming those who provide these leaders with the opportunity to leave a legacy, to do something valuable for others, and to feel good about themselves.

Are you still hesitant? Open your heart and engrave these words I heard from those whose mission is to support others' growth: *My purpose in life is to serve. I am moved by helping people; I have children, and I would like them to be treated one day in the same way I treat others; I want to leave a legacy: that my path does not end with my retirement but continues through others; For me, it is gratifying that others do not have to go through what I went through. If I figured out how to make my life easier, why wouldn't I help make life easier for others?*

If you don't have sponsors yet, I hope this chapter catalyzes you to step out of your comfort zone and take another step toward building that relationship. What action can you take to strengthen your relationship with people in positions of power and leadership? And if you already have sponsors, thank them. They need to be aware of the impact they have so they can continue doing it with others.

LESSONS LEARNED

- A sponsor will elevate your game to a completely different level. No longer will you be the only one communicating the value of your brand; you will now have an agent with great credibility and powerful social capital.

- For sponsoring to continue over time, the person who risks their social capital and name must receive a return or benefit. The relationship must be a win-win.

- We need to demonstrate the value of our work before a potential sponsor takes a risk on us.

- Rather than focusing on what we need or want to ask for, or want to ask for, it is better to create an experience in which potential mentors or sponsors feel valuable and not obligated.

- Transparency and vulnerability are part of creating that experience that will make sponsors willing to waive your brand's flag.

- Barriers to our businesses are such that we need sponsors within corporations to make our work known and to overcome bureaucratic obstacles so that we can have an opportunity to demonstrate what we are capable of doing.

- Unlearn the belief that you may be a bother or do not deserve the help of those who hold the keys to your growth. There are thousands and thousands of people whose purpose is to help others, and you can be the channel that allows them to do good.

PART IV

Rewrite the Rules

CHAPTER 14

Be part of the change

Our cultural respect for authority and hierarchy has given rise to the belief that to drive systemic change we first have to reach an executive position, become millionaires, or accumulate great power that will allow us to exercise our voice and vote. We convince ourselves that we don't have much influence if we haven't reached those spaces yet. Nothing could be further from the truth!

In our conversation, Andrew Rodríguez mentioned the *all-or-nothing syndrome*, through which we convince ourselves that if we can't enact change at a large scale, it's better to do nothing. For example, if I can't change my non-Latino leaders' thinking, why bother giving them information so they can learn more about our culture? What do I gain from that? I better stay silent. Therein lies the problem and also the opportunity.

—We don't have to change the world overnight —Andrew added—. But we can acknowledge our power to create outstanding impact in our professional space.

Systemic change will come from those at the pyramid's base, not just those at the top. That is, from the bottom up. Many of those who have reached positions of power and remain the only Latina or Latino there feel they have a lot to lose. There are exceptions, of course, but most seem more concerned with surviving in those spaces than with opening opportunities for other Latinos and Latinas. Some continue to fight against stereotypes and systemic inequities, while others assimilated so much that they seem to have disconnected from the struggles that most Latinos still face.

Change from the bottom up is inevitable if we consider how young our community is. Around 60% of Latinos and Latinas in the United States are under 33 years old. Over thirty million young Latinos will be entering or growing in professional spaces in the next decade. Because of the size of this cohort, they have unparalleled power to change how the system minimized us for hundreds of years. The youth of our Latino community is striking: the most common age among Latinos is 11 years old, compared to 58 years old for non-Latino whites. Are they feeling empowered and ready to drive change?

Less than a year ago, I traveled to El Paso, Texas, to lead a seminar at a renowned university. At a key moment in the presentation, I asked those in the room, mostly young Latinos: «What inner voice limits your actions? What voice do you hear most frequently inside your head when you want to speak up or contribute an idea?» They said things like: «I have nothing valuable to contribute,» «Who do you think you are?,» «You can't change things,» and «You're a parasite.»

On that hot and windy afternoon in El Paso, I felt sad. Here I was, in front of young Latinos under 20 years old who had grown up in spaces where we are the majority. Yet, they carried within them voices very similar to those shared with me by other Latinos in New York, Massachusetts, North Carolina, Florida, Washington, California, Chicago, and even Latin America, England, and the Netherlands.

How can we propel historic change if we carry those internal voices? Voices of disempowerment and self-judgment. Voices that mistakenly lead us to believe that we will not be able to change things. If we want to change this system that was not built with us in mind, we must embrace those human voices with compassion, love all our parts, and start acting. But how to act? Where to start changing the system?

We can start in our own space. Be part of the change by making your voice heard, letting your professional brand be known, doing your job excellently, accepting challenging opportunities, asking for what is rightfully yours, mentoring or sponsoring other Latinos, or helping correct inequities from your position and daily life. You can take countless individual actions to generate the change we want to see; many have been covered in previous chapters. In the remainder of these pages, we will evaluate how to drive change in not-so-conventional ways.

BE PART OF THE CHANGE BY TELLING YOUR STORY

Dr. Ivonne Díaz-Claisse was working as an engineer and data analyst at AT&T 16 years ago when an encounter with students helped her realize that barriers start very early for young people in our community.

—I was invited to share my story with students at a Newark, New Jersey school. That day changed my life —Ivonne told me as we had lunch together in Princeton, a few meters away from the prestigious university that bears that name—. At that event, I spoke about the barriers I had to overcome to achieve my dreams as an immigrant in a different culture. When I finished my presentation, I had a line of students waiting for my autograph —she continued with visible emotion—. They promised me they would put their best effort into their studies and continue their education since my story taught them they could succeed in this country.

That experience taught Ivonne the importance of sharing our stories with young Latinas and Latinos to open their minds to what is also possible for them and transform their internal voices of self-limitation into ones of opportunity and possibility. Committed to being part of the change, Ivonne left her job at AT&T to create and lead the non-profit organization HISPA (Hispanics Inspiring Students' Performance and Achievement).

HISPA's mission is to encourage Latino youth to discover their potential through college education, and it has committed 3,000 Latino professionals to visit schools as volunteers to tell their life stories and inspire students to believe in their abilities and dare to set ambitious goals for themselves. These students are also invited to visit companies and universities to explore their interests and experience walking through those spaces, imagining themselves there in the future. Ultimately, HISPA helps them explore possibilities different from those their parents had access to.

—Out of everything you observed or heard from our young Latinos, what was most eye-opening? —I asked Ivonne.

—I think one of the things that has moved me the most is hearing them say that they didn't know that as Latinos, they could go to college. Many believe certain opportunities are not open to us just because we are Hispanic or Latino —she replied.

Most of them were born in the United States to immigrant parents without educational opportunities, and expected for themselves the same barriers their parents faced. In their minds, Latinos don't go to college simply because those doors are not open for people like us. Moreover, many are forced to work from a young age, setting aside any college education dreams.

—Through our volunteers, many hear for the first time that they can dare to dream big. We allow them to connect with someone from our culture who embodies what can also be possible for them. In this way, they learn they can overcome the self-limiting thoughts that will show up when they set ambitious goals, especially those that no one else in their family achieved —Ivonne continued.

HISPA's work under Ivonne's leadership not only benefits students, it also helps volunteers by giving them public speaking practice and the opportunity to reconnect with their trajectory. Over time, Ivonne also realized that those visits were changing the school administrators' perception of our community.

—When they see our Latino professionals, their perception of our people changes. Their presence helps break unconscious stereotypes, and our students begin to be seen in a different light.

If you are looking for an easy and rewarding way to influence the future of our community positively, I invite you to consider volunteering for HISPA, an organization I am honored to be a part of. Sharing your story can help change the system from the bottom up, igniting the flame of possibility in our youth.

In Ivonne's words:

—Students face multiple struggles at home, so they have to understand that they need to awaken the passion for learning and growing from within themselves. For this to happen, they need to see examples of perseverance and learn that success is also possible for them, even, as some of them say, if they are Latinos.

If thousands or hundreds of thousands of us share our stories of overcoming, we will transform the future of the Latino community by replacing the ancestral messages of inferiority and disempowerment with those of possibility, achievement, and success. If you could do it, they can too. They just need to hear it from you.

ERGS, CELLS OF CULTURAL INTELLIGENCE AND ACTIVISM

In December 2023, Elon Musk proclaimed on his platform X that DEI (diversity, equity, and inclusion) policies have turned into another form of discrimination and that this practice, which has grown exponentially in recent years, must dissapear. His comment was supported by several other multimillionaires who seem to intend to stigmatize the DEI function.

In the last year, it became clear that the DEI function is ready to be reinvented so it can face the complex demands of society and the market. What had exponentially expanded as the opportunity to create greater equity in the professional world has acquired a certain stigma for being unable to solve the underlying issues. Some DEI policies have been criticized for only applying Band-Aids to a deep wound. But is that a fair assessment? Those in charge of DEI efforts have been professionals of color who, in many cases, were tasked to resolve the failures of an oppressive system and to do so with minimal support and resources, except for a few exceptions.

Given the offensive against DEI and the deep division this topic is generating, how about we look at Latino ERGs (employee resource groups) with fresh eyes? What if ERGs were not limited to being groups for social purposes and were transformed into cells of cultural intelligence and activism that helped advance the Latino cause in our organizations and professional spaces?

ERGs were born decades ago to provide spaces for socialization, connection, and support among individuals who shared affinity due to their gender, race, ethnicity, or sexual orientation, among others. This is how Latino or Hispanic ERGs were born: spaces that, in general, tend to have intense activity during Hispanic Heritage Month and less during the rest of the year.

It is common knowledge that the vast majority of these Latino ERGs struggle to be allocated a decent budget that will allow them to have continuity throughout the year. Most focus their efforts on one or two months, often inviting Latina business owners to give free seminars, classes, or talks, unable to afford their market value. Likewise, most ERG leaders are volunteers: they do not receive payment for this work and do it in their free time after an intense workday. Finally, the re-election of ERG leaders every couple of years does not help either, as the continuity of their initiatives can inevitably get lost.

—Mostly, ERGs have been a facade without true long-term impact. They are not given sufficient budget, future leaders do not emerge from ERGs, and business decisions are not made there either —a Latina woman who preferred to remain anonymous and worked for many years in the DEI space of a global corporation told me—. It makes me think that Latinos are seen as the experts in salsa, tacos, and empanadas or as the life of the party because of how fun we can be, but they do not consider us business partners. ERGs are not taken seriously and continue to be seen as a social club —this Latina executive added.

The time has come to ask ourselves if we can reposition ERGs as cells of cultural intelligence and activism. They bring unparalleled knowledge about our Latino community and market. They can contribute significant value to organizations' marketing and sales strategies, human resources strategies, and DEI strategies. In other words, it's time to assign them an educational role with strategic purposes.

After all, who better than us to understand how a Latino consumer makes purchasing decisions? According to a 2023 report by Latino Donor Collaborative (LDC), the purchasing power of the Latino community is growing twice as fast as that of non-Latino groups. What company would want to miss out on that market opportunity?

On the other hand, who better than us to understand how to attract and retain Latino talent in our organizations? Our knowledge can help make the work of human resources and DEI more effective. The same LDC report indicates that 78% of net new workers between 2020 and 2030 will be Latinos. The information on attracting and retaining this cohort resides in our ERGs.

Those who are not Latino can lack the valuable information that Latino ERGs possess and be unaware of the unique past experiences that our community went through, and that influence our work life today. Latino ERGs can become a gold mine for executives and board members, who often do not possess the detailed «insider knowledge» you and I have simply because they were not born in our shoes.

All this strategic contribution can occur within the orbit of ERGs. However, this additional work and value to the organization must be accompanied by the corresponding remuneration or recognition. It is time to eliminate the perception that ERGs are more of a hobby than a true business partner. Indeed, this «hobby» equips its leaders with important skills, such as identifying needs and opportunities, influencing executives who decide budget allocations, developing plans, managing budgets, and delegating, attracting, engaging, and retaining members. All these skills are very precious and transferable to full-time jobs.

ACT OF HEALTHY REBELLION

Reflect:

How can I influence change through my ERG? How can I transform my ERG into a key business partner and talent development channel for my organization?

_____

_____

_____

_____

If your ERG has non-Latino sponsors and access to executives within the organization, take the opportunity to influence their thinking. Help them understand how important Latinos are in organizations and the marketplace. Let them see our cultural barriers and struggles so that they can be more effective allies. Become a change agent that can help pivot the narrative. Let's not limit ourselves to being «the flavor of the month» and organizing Hispanic Heritage events that may be interesting but do not tackle the underlying issues we struggle with all year round.

BE THE CHANGE ASPIRING TO LEADERSHIP POSITIONS

Esther Aguilera has dedicated most of her professional life to driving systemic changes. Born in Jalisco, Mexico, she arrived in the United States at age 4. Daughter of undocumented parents who worked in garment manufacturing and landscaping, she experienced from a very young age what it meant to be disadvantaged and suffer systemic inequities. However, thanks to education, she discovered a different world and used her influence to create changes favoring the less privileged.

—I had the honor of working with the most powerful leaders in this country, including members of Congress and the White House, various CEOs of large corporations, and members of different boards of directors —Esther, whom I had met when she was president of LCDA (Latino Corporate Directors Association), told me.

After decades of trailblazing her way into positions of power, Esther explains it clearly:

—We can do valuable work supporting our community through different organizations, but our impact will be limited unless we have Latinas and Latinos in critical positions. We must reach those spaces; there is no option.

Through her various leadership roles and aware of the inaccurate perceptions towards our community, Esther dedicated her efforts to bringing to light how well-prepared we are for leadership positions, dispelling the myth that finding qualified Latinos and Latinas is almost impossible. Esther and other leaders with whom I connected indicated that those spaces of power we must aspire to be at are the C-Suite and boards of directors, both in non-profit and for-profit organizations.

While we can have influence and exercise our leadership in other positions that may not be as senior, there is a growing need for the voices of our Latino community in those spaces where our impact can be multiplied. However, the lack of representation of Latinas and Latinos in those places can lead us to mistakenly believe that we do not belong there, as was the case with the students who believed college was not for them, as we discussed when talking about HISPA.

Esther emphasized that Latinos and Latinas who reach positions of power are responsible for advancing and supporting others, as we will see in the next chapter.

—It's not enough for us to reach spaces of power —she said—. We must also use our position to advance our community, individually and collectively —The practice of supporting members of the same community is quite common among non-Latino groups, as we have already seen—. Supporting other Latinos in accessing executive spaces is not about being altruistic. Having more Latinos in leadership positions is good for business —she added. She also highlighted the importance of asking good questions in those spaces; for example, what percentage of the organization's purchases are allocated to women's businesses or entrepreneurs of color.

Statistics reflect all the work that remains to be done. A 2022 LCDA report indicates that approximately 70% of Fortune 1000 boards of directors, the largest one thousand companies measured in revenues, do not have a single Latino director. Not one! This is just one example of the severe representation problem we are facing. Another report that evaluated nearly one hundred companies indicates that only 7% of board members are Latino and that only 2% of executive positions are held by Latinas. While these numbers are unacceptable, we can react with anger and frustration or see them as our opportunity.

I participated in an event some time ago where I was shocked to learn that some leaders who reach executive positions or boards of directors do not know how to explain the exact path for other Latinos who come after them. This shows that there is no predetermined formula, even for those with the required talents and qualifications to reach those spaces.

At a CNBC roundtable on Latinos on Boards, one of the panelists commented:

> If you are a white man, then you remain on the «power path.» The power path comprises a series of positions that lead to the executive ranks. On the other hand, too many people of color are being diverted to what I call the «cul-de-sac» strategy. They are promoted to a position that then leads nowhere. Then, if they want to continue growing, they are asked to take a lower position in another department to eventually move up again.

Our path is not clear and may have more detours than necessary as we are asked time and time again to prove that we can occupy those spaces of power. Another panel participant noted: «Those who aspire to reach those positions must ensure they accumulate work experiences that demonstrate significant strategic contributions because boards of directors generally look for people who add significant value.» He added that «anything you can do to show that you have made a difference in advancing an organization is a great differentiator.» Keep this in mind when choosing which projects to take on. Evaluate whether they are within the «power path» or if they represent a *cul-de-sac*. Also, remember to keep a record of all your achievements.

Another panelist recommended being strategic in acquiring the skills required to succeed in those spaces, such as knowing how to handle different personalities, developing the power to influence their decision-making, bringing conflictive discussions to a successful conclusion, and creating consensus. As we have seen in this book, some key pieces for your success include thoroughly understanding your audience, anticipating the benefits they seek, and creating the space for their voices to be expressed and heard. These skills can begin to be practiced from the beginning of your career and in ERGs. In addition, if in your childhood you were a translator for your parents, it's possible that at some point you had to influence others. Every experience counts and is valuable. Do not overlook or disqualify it because others did not have it.

Finally, the CNBC panelists and those interviewed for this book agreed that their relationships were key to accessing those spaces, particularly with mentors and sponsors. In Esther Aguilera's words, «It's not so much about what you know, but who you know.» Let's continue to build our networks, as that is how we will mainly pave the way to leadership positions.

Tell your story, elevate your ERGs mission, and fearlessly aspire to leadership positions because we belong there, too. We can be change agents wherever we find ourselves. When I feel frustrated because my efforts don't seem to bear fruit, I remind myself of what Rumi, the great Sufi poet, said: «You are not a drop in the ocean; you are the ocean in a drop.»

LESSONS LEARNED

- The concept of change in the hands of the «small individual» can be difficult for Latinos to accept due to the deep-rooted respect for hierarchies we have historically carried.

- Sharing our stories with our young people can open their minds to what is possible for them and help transform their internal voices of disempowerment into ones of opportunity and possibility.

- The time has come to ask ourselves if we can reposition ERGs as cells of cultural intelligence and activism by assigning them an educational role with strategic purposes.

- Latino ERGs can become a goldmine for executives and board members, who often lack the detailed knowledge you and I possess simply because they have never been in our shoes.

- The impact of our work will be limited unless we have Latinas and Latinos in key positions. We must reach those spaces; there is no option.

- If you were your parents' translators in childhood, it is possible that at some point you had to influence others in positions of power. Every experience is useful and valuable. Do not overlook or disqualify it just because others have not had it.

CHAPTER 15

Push up and pull up

Every significant change in trajectory generally occurs after a turning point. This is usually an important event that charts a new destiny for a path that seemed to be predetermined. We have seen it happen at various moments in history. For example, the invention of the printing press created a before and after in access to information and knowledge. The printing press was a significant turning point. Later, the arrival of the internet in our homes generated a new turning point that further expanded access to information. You may have experienced a turning point in your life as well. Certain events create such radical changes that it may be difficult to imagine what life was like before they occurred.

Our Latino community is on the brink of an imminent turning point, a historic moment of change after which our exponential growth will be such that it will be hard for future generations to understand the circumstances of inequality in which we have lived. For this turning point to finally materialize, we must take a definite step forward in transforming our mindsets. Although we have been becoming increasingly aware of the power we have and that many statistics reflect, we still need to embrace that each one of us, as individuals, has the power to transform the spaces in which we are immersed.

I find that we often behave like visitors rather than established citizens of this country, and it sometimes seems we are waiting for someone else to lead the change we wish to see. For example, *Things will change for us when a Latino or Latina becomes president; We need more Latinos in Hollywood to influence culture and mindsets in that space; We need a sports star who will advocate for us to be finally on the radar;* and *We depend on allies sponsoring more Latinas to reach positions of power.*

These ways of thinking rob us of the responsibility and opportunity to be change agents. My conversation with Andrew Rodriguez was revealing in that sense. In his own words:

—Expecting others who reach leadership spaces to carry out the changes we want to see is a recipe for disaster. We must lead the change at every step, from our place. Today, you can accept your role as a change agent and let that way of being become part of your identity, habits, role, and purpose. Once you reach a leadership position, everything will be easier because you will already be a catalyst for change.

Our historic turning point will not come from the hand of a mighty savior who will change our lives but from the grassroots, from the trenches. It will happen when you, me, thousands, and millions of Latinas accept with conviction that we are the change we have been waiting for.

If you are ready to embrace your role and create meaningful change for our community, I invite you to consider that as you reach new spaces and break through the glass ceiling, you can extend a hand to those climbing and rising. This is called *push-up and pull-up,* and it's about using your talents, experiences, knowledge, and social capital to lift and sponsor other Latinas as you grow. In other words, this is a commitment to demonstrate a different behavior from the one that has held us back the most: not helping each other enough or turning our backs on one another.

UNDERSTANDING WHAT LIES BEHIND THE REFUSAL TO HELP EACH OTHER

Our colonial mindset

Our colonization process culminated with the establishment of systemic poverty, lack of opportunities, and widespread barriers in our countries. Operating in survival, we adopted particular mindsets and ways of thinking that, over time, became our belief system. Among these mindsets, we find scarcity *(There is not enough space or opportunities for everyone)*, survival *(I can barely keep up in this space where I am a minority. I don't have enough energy to help others)*, machismo *(I can trust a man for this important job, but not so much a woman)*, and envy *(I can't allow her to keep advancing! What if I am left behind?)*.

If we continue to drag these ancestral mindsets and remain unaware of how they influence our thinking, feelings, and behavior, we will stay trapped in a past that no longer aligns with the opportunities ahead.

Being the only one

For some time now, I have heard «*I am the only Latina in my space*» at various events and conferences. That is, the only Latina executive in my company, the only Latina entrepreneur in this business incubator, the only Latina on this board of directors, the only Latina to receive capital from these investors... and so on. Feeling proud of being the only Latina in certain spaces is natural after all the hard work we put into breaking those glass ceilings. Still, when being the only one borders on territoriality, it becomes detrimental to our collective progress.

If you are the only Latina in your space, ask yourself how you would feel if another Latina suddenly arrived. Would you feel threatened? Would you start competing to prove who is better and who deserves to be there? This happens more frequently than we think. A part of ourselves can fear being displaced from the power groups that have accepted us. In those spaces, we can become the reference point for our community, and with the arrival of a second Latina, our insecurities and scarcity mindsets may be unleashed. We then begin to act territorially, perhaps even feeling the need to push the other woman out of our way.

—Among the executives in my workplace, there was only one Latina woman —said a Latina leader who asked to remain anonymous—. I tried to connect with her for years and ask for mentorship, but I always found a closed door. In the meantime, I had several non-Latino mentors, developed an excellent relationship with the firm's executives, and continued to grow in my career. After a reorganization, this Latina woman became my boss! It was the most challenging experience I have ever had in my professional life. I felt like I was immersed in a forced relationship. A few months after being assigned to her team, she got me fired from the company where I had worked for more than a decade —after a pause, she added—: I confess that it felt like a relief; it was a liberation.

Wanting to be the only Latina and fearing that another may overshadow our shine can lead us to turn our backs on other Latinas and cut off their progress into our territory. Therefore, whenever I hear someone say, «I'm the only Latina in my space,» I want to ask them: «What are you doing to stop being the only one?»

The stigma of helping a sister

There is a penalty for helping those who look like us, which can lead us to stop helping other Latinas and Latinos for fear of being unfavorably rated if others notice that we prioritize sponsoring other Latinos. A Harvard Business Review article titled «Women and Minorities Are Penalized for Promoting Diversity» describes how women are viewed suspiciously when we promote diversity in our professional spaces. Specifically, women and minorities who supported people like them received lower performance ratings. In other words, by helping our own, we can be perceived as less skilled to do our jobs.

This negative impact on how our talents and potential are perceived contributes to the fact that 85% of corporate executives and board members are still white men. They do not face the same stigma when they promote other white men.

As we achieve a critical mass of Latinos supporting other Latinos, we can gradually normalize this behavior. In the meantime, we must face our fears and move forward by helping our own. If not you, then who? And if not now, then when?

The unaware leader

This came up during a conversation with a Latina friend, a prominent and award-winning executive with decades of experience, who was in the process of looking for a job at the time of writing this book.

—I connected with several Latinas in very high positions in their industry —she told me—. When I asked for their help in my job search process, they limited themselves to recommending how to continue looking for a job. But they did not use their social capital to connect me with other executives in their circle.

While we can open doors and sponsor other Latinas, we often fail to do so because we have yet to fully acknowledge our power. We are unaware of our influence. It is possible that, used to running around and surviving, we remain trapped in a hamster wheel, not fully realizing that we are now in a space from which we can rewrite the game's rules.

So, when you knock on doors that don't open or don't open how you would have liked, consider that the person in front of you may not yet be aware of all they can do.

IN SEARCH OF OUR CHANGE AGENTS

To write this section, I decided to experiment: I went out to find our change agents at in-person events and on social media. For months, I looked for professionals who had helped other Latinas and Latinos as they moved up, those who risked the social capital they had built to promote the advancement of others in our community. I wanted to understand how they think and why they are willing to take risks for others. What drives them to do it? Why are there few like them in our community?

If we multiply these change agents in all spaces and hierarchical levels, we will reach the tipping point that our community needs. We will break the glass ceiling and write a new story of collective progress. My first question to them was: What drives you to help another Latina or Latino? Why do you do it? This is what they responded:

> When I became aware of our value and the power we possess and noticed our absence in positions of authority, I decided to take action. Being the only Latina in my space led me to ask myself: if I made it to this level, how can I help others reach it, too?
>
> Helping other Latinos is my vocation and life purpose. It is not easy and can be frustrating, but looking at our progress so far, I can confidently say that my actions have had a positive impact.
>
> Lending a hand to others is a value I learned at home by observing my parents. We didn't have anything to spare, but there was always enough to help those who needed it. I want to continue with that legacy.
>
> How could I look at myself in the mirror knowing that I let pass an opportunity to help our people grow?
>
> We must act with determination when helping our own. How can we expect others to do the same if we don't?
>
> Nothing is more beautiful than seeing your people express gratitude because you were there when they needed you the most.

These individuals do not measure their success simply by advancing their careers, only to find themselves lonely at the top. Instead, they choose to open doors of opportunity to other Latinas and Latinos from their current positions, even if they are not that senior yet, believing that we can all grow together. In the following pages, we will delve deeper into their lives. Will you join me?

«WE DON'T HAVE ENOUGH LATINAS TO PROMOTE»

J. C. González-Mendez caught my attention during an event at the United Nations. As a panelist, he shared how he had heard repeatedly that McDonald's, his employer, did not have enough college-educated Latinas to be promoted to managerial positions. He decided to lead the change and moved heaven and earth to launch the first internship program focused on Latinas, paving the way for their executive careers.

—I had recently started my career with the company and repeatedly heard that finding qualified Latinas to be promoted to managerial and executive positions was difficult. I decided to launch a part-time program that employed Latina college students.

J. C., the oldest of three brothers and four sisters, grew up surrounded by women. Throughout his career, most of his mentors had been women. He was aware of our work ethic and potential, as well as our conscientiousness, discipline, and loyalty. For this reason, he decided to put his career on the line and become the gateway for Latina women to demonstrate what they were capable of.

His internship program was revolutionary, particularly for the parents of the Latina students he hired. The first step was working in a restaurant's kitchen to gain a solid understanding of business operations. Because of this, the program encountered resistance from some parents who were opposed to their college-educated daughters cooking hamburgers.

—I first had to convince the Human Resources manager about the value of this program, and then I had to convince our interns' parents —he told me—. I understood their resistance because when I decided to continue my career in the company's operations area, my mom practically ate me alive. She asked, «Is this what all our sacrifice to send you to college was for? For you to be cooking hamburgers?» J. C. did not doubt that the resistance came from not understanding the opportunities with career progression. And what did he do? He invited all families to the office on a Sunday and explained the program in detail, showing real numbers of employees who had continued their careers at McDonald's and were now participating in the company's profit-sharing program.

But that was not all.

—There was a young intern named Ofelia, whose mother did not seem very convinced at that meeting —J. C. continued—, so I invited the mother and her daughter to have dinner with my wife and showed them my shares and participation in the company's profits. I showed the mother what was possible for Ofelia if she worked with us. I wanted that type of opportunity for our people. We could no longer afford to be left out.

The impact on Ofelia's mother was profound. From that day on, whenever her daughter had opportunities to advance at work, she would suggest to Ofelia, «Ask J. C. and see what he thinks.»

Ofelia Kumpf, whom I also connected with to hear her side of this story, completed the internship program, rose through the company ranks, and recently retired as Vice President and General Manager responsible for restaurants in five states. After thirty years at McDonald's, at the time of her retirement, she was the highest-ranked Latina in the United States and globally.

—Sponsorship is vital for women, especially us —Ofelia told me—. J. C. was my coach, mentor, and sponsor throughout my career. It was a relationship built on trust, not disappointing the other person, and speaking the truth to each other —J. C.'s impact on Ofelia's career was significant. Over time, his demonstrated values and standards inspired Ofelia to do the same—. I took on the responsibility of showing in my day-to-day work the values that I brought from home and that were important to me, such as expressing my opinions and supporting the growth of others, especially other Latinas.

J.C. was a pioneer in creating opportunities for Latina women in an organization where we were underrepresented in executive positions. His actions also changed internal perceptions about Latino talent and opened the minds of the interns' families regarding what was possible for their daughters. J.C. was a change agent in his company and the lives of numerous families. Thanks to his program, J.C.'s region ranked among the top five in earnings nationwide. Additionally, 72% of his managers were Latino, and half of those were women when only a few years earlier, Latinas were a tiny minority. Many continued their path to managerial and executive positions. With a career spanning more than three decades in the company, J.C. retired after serving several years as President of Latin America and as global President of the Ronald McDonald Foundation.

At the end of our meeting, and thinking about the research report that explains we are punished for promoting diversity, I asked him:

—Were you ever fearful of being judged for focusing on helping our people? Were you afraid of what others would think?

—If we want change to happen, we must act with determination and move forward without apologizing because supporting our people is the right thing to do; it's the right thing! —he emphasized—. Besides, who better than ourselves to know the talent, work ethic and loyalty of our people? I couldn't look at myself in the mirror and feel good about myself, knowing I lost the opportunity to do something for our community because of what people might say! If people will speak badly because we did the right thing, so be it!

IT TAKES ONE TO CREATE A NEW CULTURE

In the adventure of finding our change agents, I created a post on LinkedIn inviting those who had helped other Latinas break glass ceilings or those who had received such help to connect with me so they could tell me their stories.

The numbers I will share speak for themselves. That post had about 12,000 views and more than a hundred interactions, but only a few interviews emerged. It felt like looking for a needle in a haystack. One of those interviewees was Teri Arvesú González, an executive at a leading media company who shared the story of another Latina executive, Jessica Rodriguez, who had a significant impact on her career and on that of many other Latinas, so much so that a new culture emerged from her actions.

—Jessica not only created a Council of Women Leaders, providing tangible opportunities for visibility and growth to many Latinas, but she also became an active mentor and sponsor and taught us to support each other instead of reinforcing the stereotype that we have to compete —Teri told me. In other words, Jessica changed many Latina women's career trajectories and worked to change their mindsets. During her time at the company, she left a legacy of collaboration and support over the need to compete and feel envy.

Teri added:

—When a woman with Jessica's track record and professional caliber decides to change a culture, she charts a path other women will want to follow. Watching her fight for resources to support the growth of other women or seeing her actively mentoring and sponsoring was something that many of us incorporated as a model of what would be expected from us when we reached her level.

A few days later, I connected with Jessica herself.

—I wanted to create enthusiasm about helping other women and make it popular to support each other's growth in the organization —she told me warmly while firmly—. I was intentional about building that legacy.

—Why did you take on tasks that weren't part of your annual performance evaluation? Where did that strong desire to help others come from? —I asked her.

—I was always driven by a sense of purpose, mission, and duty —she asserted and told me how her father and mother, immigrants who had left everything behind to immerse into a new culture, had instilled in her that if you received a lot, you also have the responsibility to give a lot. They would tell her—. We expect a lot from you because we made many sacrifices to get to where we are.

And so, she did, seeking to honor her parents' sacrifice.

—I also had my angels on earth. Many of my opportunities came when someone believed in me at times when I didn't even believe in myself. Some people changed the trajectory of my career and my life —she said. Those angels took many forms. From her sixth-grade teacher who told her that she should apply to a particular music program that opened doors for her, to her college professors who encouraged her to work in investment banking, an industry she knew nothing about, to men at her job who sponsored her and guided her path. There were many angels—. Someone did it for me, and I wanted to do it for others.

Early on, Jessica understood that helping other women was a choice she could make in her daily life and that her decision would depend on whether she viewed the world through a lens of abundance or scarcity.

—We carry the dilemma of helping others because we have been instilled with the zero-sum game —she added—. In this game, if I win, you lose. There is only room for one or a few, so I better take care of what's mine, focus on my career, and let others figure things out as they go —Jessica did not want to be like that and decided to do it differently—. It's like when a train will depart from the station, and doors are about to close. I like to keep the doors open and see how many women I can take with me.

Finally, and very similar to J. C. González-Mendez, Jessica dared to promote her ideals.

—To be successful, you have to take risks —she told me. Perhaps she developed her strength after losing her father at the age of 15. Jessica had to become a negotiator and translator for her widowed mother, who was in charge of four children. She spoke with the bank manager when they received a deposit, translated parent-teacher conferences for her mother, and advocated for the needs of her loved ones—. Those are tremendous qualities that you then bring to your company.

She is absolutely right.

THE GREATNESS OF GIVING IN SILENCE

If giving what is yours to help and sponsor others is an act of greatness, imagine how honorable it is when that act remains so secret that not even the person who benefits from it knows who helped her.

That is the story of Diana Peña, a Human Resources executive who never received support from a sponsor during her career but did not hesitate for a second when faced with the opportunity to sponsor another Latina woman. She kept it a secret because she knew that would be better for everyone involved.

One of her company employees, Ivonne, typed a comment in the chat during a virtual meeting with the company's CEO and his executive team to discuss career topics.

—She wrote that it would be essential to consider those who change jobs without changing roles —said Diana—. I didn't quite understand what Ivonne meant, but her comment stayed with me —Ivonne had been on Diana's radar for some time—. She first caught my attention on social media. I thought, «She's

Latina, like me,» then I realized we worked at the same company —Besides being an outstanding employee who exceeded her objectives, Ivonne was very involved in helping our community. None of that went unnoticed by Diana—. Something didn't sit right with me because even though Ivonne seemed to be valued for her work and created an impact in the community, her name had never been mentioned at the tables where promotions and salary increases were discussed. That caught my attention —Diana observed—. It's time to look under the hood, I told myself.

Looking into her work history, Diana noticed that Ivonne had been with the firm for eight years, six of which she had remained at the same level. Before Diana joined the firm, Ivonne had been moved with her boss about three times within the organization, yet despite the fact that her boss had been promoted in position and salary, Ivonne had not received the same treatment. In other words, she was given more responsibility but not with an updated position and salary.

Diana decided to meet with Ivonne's boss to understand the situation. He told her:

—I proposed a generous salary increase for her several times because her work consistently exceeds objectives. But each time, the increase was denied. Ivonne was disappointed and didn't take it well, but I did everything possible.

At that moment, Diana understood what had happened. Ivonne had reached the top of her category, earning the maximum possible salary for her level. Her boss had been focused on getting her more money when the solution lay in reclassifying Ivonne's job.

—I could not let more time pass, so I decided to take this case into my own hands —Diana told me—. I got Ivonne moved up two bands higher and increased her salary to six figures. And when it was time to communicate this good news to Ivonne, I asked her boss to do it. I didn't want Ivonne to know I was involved because that could affect her relationship with her boss.

Diana also approved an exception so Ivonne could enroll in a six-month coaching program for high-potential individuals. Diana stayed behind the scenes while Ivonne's boss communicated these opportunities. In addition, she sponsored Ivonne for a leadership position in the firm's ERG, where Diana was the executive advisor. This would allow Ivonne to gain more visibility with the leaders.

—As I am her mentor and coach, she recently called me and asked me if I was behind all of this because she felt that I had been her sponsor —Diana told me. Diana found a way to excuse herself and avoid answering. So, if Ivonne is reading this book, this will be the first time she becomes aware of all Diana did to fix what was unfair. This will be the first time that Diana's actions become public.

—Why did you do it? —I asked her.

Because someone had to do something. We had an unfair situation that had to be corrected, and I decided to be the one to do it. After a brief pause, she added:

—Maybe it concerns my dad, whom I lost in 2021. Throughout his life, he told me that when I was the only one who looked a certain way in the room, I had to remember that I was as smart and qualified as others —Diana said, with visible emotion—. He taught me to have my voice, to develop my strength, and to know my worth. And that's what it's about: putting our strength and talents to use for the advancement of our community.

Perhaps it's no coincidence that Diana, Jennifer, and J. C. all lost loved ones who were pillars in their lives, and as a result, they faced obstacles that made them stronger from an early age. Maybe pain can indeed make us stronger. Using that strength to benefit others is noble, even when we aren't asked to.

Our collective growth and the extent to which it accelerates depend on your sponsorship of other Latinas and Latinos. Push up and pull up! Please consider taking that step today to build your legacy.

ACT OF HEALTHY REBELLION

Reflect on:

How can I use the challenges I faced to support other Latinas? Am I willing to use my social capital to sponsor another Latina?

_____

_____

_____

_____

_____

LESSONS LEARNED

- Our historic turning point will not come from the hand of a powerful savior, but it will start from the trenches. It will happen when you, I, thousands, and then millions of Latinas accept that we are the change agents we have been waiting for.

- As you break through the glass ceiling, you can turn around and extend a hand to those climbing up. This is known as push-up and pull up.

- Wanting to be the only Latina in our spaces or fearing that another Latina will overshadow our shine can lead us to turn our backs on others. That's why, every time I hear someone say, «I'm the only Latina in my space,» I want to ask them, «What are you doing to stop being the only one?»

- We may be accustomed to running around in survival mode, getting trapped in a hamster wheel, without realizing that we have already reached a space from where we can rewrite the rules of the game.

- If we multiply our change agents in all spaces and hierarchical levels, we will reach the turning point that our community seeks. We will normalize the behavior of helping other Latinos, break the glass ceiling, and write a new story of collective progress.

- Early on, Jessica understood that helping other women was a choice she could make in her daily life and that her decision to do so would depend on whether she viewed the world through a lens of abundance or one of scarcity.

- If we want to see meaningful change, we must act with determination and move forward without apologizing. Supporting our people is our responsibility and an impactful way to build a legacy.

CHAPTER 16

Our unity, a utopia?

Regardless of whether we help other Latinas here and there, is our unity as a community possible? How can we make it happen? I'm referring to the type of unity that invites a mindset change, one in which we see ourselves as part of a larger cohort where what brings us together overshadows our differences.

What would happen if the Latino community pushed in one direction, no longer behaving like crabs in a bucket but as members of the same extended family, sharing our knowledge, sponsoring each other, supporting our entrepreneurs, and accelerating our arrival to spaces of power where the rules of the game are written? What would happen if we saw other community members through the eyes of opportunity and not through the lens of competition and separation?

With those same questions, I went out into the world and encountered a bit of everything. It seems ironic, but we are divided in our opinions on whether we can ever be united.

—It isn't easy. To start, look at the division we have between Democrats and Republicans within the Latino community. How can we ever unite if we think so differently about the fundamental pillars of our society and economy? —a Latina executive with Cuban roots questioned.

—I think we made quite a bit of progress, although we still have a long way to go —a Mexican-rooted executive said.

—We are still very connected to our countries of origin, and those cultural differences are almost insurmountable —a Dominican entrepreneur noted.

—Not supporting each other seems like a microaggression to me. How many years or generations will it take us to transform that lack of interest in supporting our community? Too many, perhaps —lamented an entrepreneur of Puerto Rican roots, pointing out her weariness and frustration.

—Actually, I believe it's possible. In our city, we formed a group of Latina leaders and meet frequently to help each other —a director of a non-profit organization in Charlotte, North Carolina, told me.

Each bell rang in its way, many expressing their doubts and some believing in the possibility of something different.

OUR DIVERSITY, AT THE ROOTS OF OUR DIVISION

Our diversity runs deep and wide. We are a melting pot of races, cultures, languages, socioeconomic levels, and degrees of acculturation. Similarly, we may think differently about important issues that influence our worldview and define the rules of our society. Just as a test, ask a group of Latinas and Latinos what they think about illegal immigration from our countries and prepare to receive a variety of responses. Don't be surprised if someone who crossed the border without papers in the past is now fervently opposed to others arriving by the same means. Our diversity of opinions can be even more evident with other issues, such as gay marriage, child adoption by same-sex couples, the legalization of marijuana, and more. Get ready for a diversity of opinions, even within the same family. Given where we are, how will it ever be possible for us to unite as a community?

—When our company's LGBTQIA+ community had clear objectives, it made progress —a Latina corporate executive told me—. But the effort was diluted when we diversified too much into more specific subgroups. I then understood the importance of common goals. Without them, it's tough to advance a cause.

What would that common cause be for our Latino community? And can we set common goals behind which we can all align? After all, is there anything louder and more disorderly than an open debate among Latinos and Latinas?

LOOK AT THOSE WHO ADVANCED BECAUSE THEY WERE UNITED

For some years now, many of us observed the progress of the African American community, which united in a common cause after the murder of George Floyd. The results were tangible in several areas, including access to leadership positions, boards of directors, promotions to C-suite, and contracts with African American entrepreneurs. A *Wall Street Journal* article indicates that for every one hundred men promoted for the first time in 2021, 72 were African American. Progress was also noted in hiring efforts and in the promotion of African American professionals to the highest ranks. In 2021, eight African Americans were CEOs in Fortune 500 companies, compared to only four a year earlier, demonstrating ambitious goals to advance African American talent.

Although these efforts slowed down over time, we have much to learn. We have seen a different pace of progress in the Latino cohort than in the African American community. That's why I have been asking myself for some time now and have also inquired about it publicly at conferences and events: What can we learn from our African American brothers and sisters to close the systemic gaps for Latinos? I believe there is much to learn, starting with how they support one another.

Sol Trujillo, CEO, entrepreneur, investor, founder of Latino Donor Collaborative, and co-founder of L'ATTITUDE, offered an additional point of view on the Jewish community.

—Have you seen how Jewish people help each other? —he asked during our conversation—. They invest in other Jews, buy from other Jews, recommend each other for jobs, and support each other as if they were family. We have a lot to learn from them.

The Jewish community is also diverse, but their unity is stronger than their differences. Its members come from different countries, speak different languages, and are multiracial, with at least 15% of people of color within the community. The support they provide to one another comes from understanding that their unity allowed them to survive over time and is one of their most prominent religious and cultural values.

—We are so focused on our differences that we don't act as a group — Sol added—. It's vital that we unite and that, instead of competing, we do as people of the Jewish faith do. For them, if there are three who are successful, I can be the fourth, and those three can help me achieve it. That is the mentality we need.

I heard something similar regarding the Hindu and Japanese communities. Their members seem to help each other more than Latinos do.

As we continue to explore this topic, I want us to envision a revolutionary concept. Because we are one of the most diverse communities in the United States, we can become a role model of unity in diversity. Given the division and intolerance that plague our society, if we figure out how to overcome our racial, cultural, linguistic, and educational differences, we can become a beacon of what is possible for the rest of the United States and the world.

Have you noticed that our genetics carry something of all other communities? Just considering race and skin color, among Latinos and Latinas you will find individuals with different degrees of Native American, African, Anglo, and Asian ancestry, groups our society perceives as different. In a way, we bring them all together in our collective. Imagine what could be possible if we learn to function harmoniously in our diversity. We can become a success story that defies the narrative of those who continue to find separation in diversity.

OUR DIVERSITY, OPPORTUNITY FOR UNITY

While it is true that our diversity has caused division, it also invites us to work harder to find that which unites us. When the emphasis has been placed on our visible differences, it is our task to dig deeper into our essence to find what brings us together.

The first steps towards our unity can be found within each of us and require a change in how we see our collective. We must believe that our unity is possible and try to find what unites us. This is similar to what we covered earlier about seeking common ground with allies who look different from us. Finding those common points will make it easier for us to support each other. Therefore, if you want more unity among Latinas, it is imperative that the next time you have another Latina in front of you, no matter how different she looks or sounds, you set out to go beyond the differences to find what you have in common, even if at first it seems to be not much.

For most of my professional life, I found myself trailblazing spaces where only a few were Latina and Latino. My experience of immersion in our culture and community happened later on, thanks to a professional opportunity that gave a turn to my way of thinking. Working closely with hundreds of Latino entrepreneurs, I experienced firsthand what we have in common. I was surrounded by such diversity, and my thirst for belonging was so deep that I intentionally focused on finding common ground. As I did so, I began to feel at home for the first time since my arrival to the United States.

When you focus on finding what unites us, you realize it is much more than what you initially thought, but getting there requires a firm intention to go beyond initial impressions. In the following pages, I will share what points of unity in our diversity I found, which invited me to dream that a more united community is possible.

In my heart, I firmly believe it is.

VALUES WE LEARNED FROM OUR CULTURE

—I went to Cartagena for three days with an Australian neighbor, and it turned out to be a revealing experience —Sara, a Colombian friend and an executive at one of the most important banks in the country, shared with me—, I got to see my own culture through the eyes of a foreigner, and it was fascinating.

—Tell me, what did you notice? What struck you the most? —I asked, eager to compare notes and experiences.

—My neighbor kept commenting on how, in her culture, people tend to be colder or more reserved, while in Cartagena, you find people who possess less in a material sense but who are very warm. They wouldn't stop smiling at her, and that touched her heart. She had an unforgettable experience.

I understood perfectly well what she was referring to. Have you ever met an Anglo who visited our countries and disliked the experience? I haven't. Everyone I know who has visited our culture returns delighted with the food, the music, and, above all, our people. Isn't that right? Our warmth, generosity, and joy characterize us. We know about human connection and building relationships from our human essence, and this touches the other person's heart. We are masters at making others feel at home in unfamiliar spaces. We value the group, the collective, the tribe, family, and friends, so we are also very loyal to those groups that welcome us in their circle. Our loyalty and our commitment to our work are unmatched.

Our culture instilled in us these essential values that are part of what I call the culture of the heart, which I will cover in more depth in the next chapter. I, from Argentina, and you, from your country of origin as an immigrant or with your ancestry as the daughter of Latino immigrants, share those values. They are imprinted in our being and essence.

During my professional immersion in the Latino community, leading entrepreneurship centers and incubators, that was the first thing I noticed: we have a lot of values in common. Our warmth, joy, and group thinking are all part of who we are. And when we connect with others through those heart-centered values, it becomes easier to want to support them; we feel them as our own.

Next time you are in front of another Latina or Latino with whom you feel a certain separation, intentionally find those shared values, perhaps allowing yourself to be the first to embody and demonstrate them. If you allow yourself to be warm, joyful, and generous, showing more of your essence, you will give the other person the space and freedom to do the same. Once a deeper and genuine connection has occurred, it will be easier to want to support one another with our goals. Give it a try!

OUR SHARED EXPERIENCES AND STRUGGLES

As my immersion in our community continued, I noticed other similarities with other Latinos and Latinas that were not so evident in the beginning.

—Next week, I have a meeting with an executive at a potential client, and I'm terrified of showing up —Joanna, born here to Puerto Rican parents and owner of a professional services firm, told me.

—Why? —I asked with curiosity. Before this private coaching session with me, Joanna had shown up as one of the strongest and most extroverted people in the entrepreneurship class. I was quite shocked to hear her doubt herself in this way.

—Because he's a white man, and I will feel uncomfortable talking about money and negotiating my prices. I usually get so overwhelmed that I start my negotiation by offering a discount they never requested. I want to close the deal and leave as soon as possible.

I listened in silence as Joanna told me how her hands shook badly on those opportunities, skyrocketing her anxiety. «But...,» I thought, «that's precisely how I feel on those occasions. And, like her, I end up charging less for my work.»

It didn't matter that Joanna had been an entrepreneur for years and that I came from a corporate space. It also didn't matter that we were born in different countries and grew up in different cultures, nor that I had an accent and Joanna spoke perfect English. Our struggles and the barriers we faced were quite similar. Identical situations arose when talking with other Latino entrepreneurs and later on with Latino employees of organizations and corporations where I worked as a consultant. What I noticed is that although diverse, there were many similarities in the barriers we face, not only when it comes to charging our worth but also in the use of our voice, in how we can freeze when advocating for ourselves, in the inner voices that get triggered when we feel we don't belong, and much more. Something was happening here, and it was worth further investigating. Needless to say, because of existing systemic bias and racism, Afro-Latinos, LGBTQIA+ in our community, neurodivergent Latinos and Latinas, etc., face additional barriers because of these intersections.

I embarked on a mission to understand how much of our experiences we had in common and whether those could become fertile ground for our unity. Because of how painful some of our past experiences have been, I knew it was going to be difficult to have others open up and talk. We carry our problems and struggles in silence, keeping them to ourselves, whether out of fear or shame or because we somehow believe we must show we are strong. However, one question was enough to touch those hearts and let a torrent of words pour out.

«Tell me about yourself. How did you get here? What events would you say marked your life the most?» was the first question I posed to dozens of Latinas I interviewed. In more than half of these encounters, we cried. Remembering where we come from and the sacrifice of our loved ones was very moving. In many other cases, we come face to face with our frustration or fatigue because the barriers we encounter are still numerous, and the energy to keep breaking them seems to wane.

No matter who I had in front of me: corporate employees, entrepreneurs, white Latinas, brown Latinas, Afro-Latinas, immigrants, daughters of migrants, non-binary Latinas, married, single, in a relationship, speaking in Spanish, in English, in both languages, conversation after conversation I noticed similarities that bring us together in a very intimate way, but that we can be unaware of or ignore as we focus on working hard without allowing ourselves to talk about what we carry.

In getting to know our untold stories lies the secret of our unity.

Those who immigrated share the never-ending pain of an uprooting we never healed. We share the experience of having gone through a cultural shock that plunged us without warning into a different reality, one that sometimes feels like a movie because it doesn't seem real. We share working in spaces that seem too impersonal or sometimes hostile, so different from what we remember from our homelands. We share counting the days to hug our family again, the one we left behind in our home countries, a dream that for some is unattainable.

Those born in the United States who still carry their ancestors' traumatic immigration experiences share memories of a childhood in which they had to grow up too fast, became the voice of parents who did not know the culture or speak the language, and in some cases, took on the role of their caretakers from a young age. They share living in one culture at home and in a different one at work, with a foot in each space and trying to move successfully through both. They share feelings of internal and external pressure to achieve something greater than what their ancestors had access to, striving to honor their stories and prove that their sacrifice was worth it after all.

When was the last time you allowed yourself to be vulnerable and asked another Latina woman, «How did you get to where you are? What events marked your life most deeply?»

Our stories are the gateway to our unity when narrated and listened to from the heart. We will only achieve true unity if we know our history and realize we are still carrying each other through our healing process.

ACT OF HEALTHY REBELLION

In the next 48 hours, approach a person from our community with whom you feel separation or division. Learn about their story, their barriers, and their lessons learned.

Don't deprive yourself of the magic of creating micro-moments of unity with other Latinas and Latinos because, in those moments, you will find that it is in our minds that most barriers and divisions exist.

LESSONS LEARNED

- We have not seen the same pace of progress in the Latino community as in the African American community. What can we learn from them to close the systemic gaps for Latinos?

- As Latinos, we can become role models if we find a way to unite in our marked diversity.

- Our diversity invites us to work harder to find what unites us.

- If you want more unity among Latina women, it is imperative that when you have one in front of you, you try hard to find the things that you have in common, even if they may seem few at first.

- If you give yourself permission to be warm, joyful, and generous, showing your essence, you will provide the person in front of you the freedom to do the same.

- When narrated and listened to from the heart, our stories are the gateway to our unity. We will not be able to achieve solid and true unity without realizing that what unites us is much greater than what separates us.

- Do not deprive yourself of the magic of creating micro-moments of unity with other Latinas and Latinos because, in them, you will find that most of the time, the barriers and divisions only exist in our minds.

CHAPTER 17

Create the third culture

As we allow our authentic cultural essence to come to light, as we heal our self-esteem, appreciate who we are, and demonstrate the values of our culture, we will not only positively impact our organizations and communities but also contribute to transforming the very foundations of American society.

In the coming decades, we will experience an unprecedented cultural fusion. You, me, and millions of Latinos will have the opportunity to demonstrate the best of our culture, the culture of the heart, which, in synch with the culture of the mind, will allow us to advance our country to spaces of cooperation and unity unknown until now.

Going from feeling ignored or dismissed to leading an unprecedented historical change may seem like a fantasy. Be ready to be surprised. Creating a new culture that combines the best of the cultures of the heart and mind has already taken its first steps.

THE CULTURES OF THE MIND AND THE HEART

In our society and the broader world, we find two distinct and differentiated cultures: the culture of the mind and the culture of the heart.

The culture of the mind is characterized by materialization on the physical plane. Technological and scientific advances and a focus on results, profits, efficiency, and productivity characterize it. Success metrics center on achieving material results. This type of culture can predominate in developed countries, mostly Anglo-Saxon, where leadership is represented by masculine energy, not because of gender, but because of its focus on logic and action.

On the other hand, the culture of the heart is characterized by its connection with the intangible. Spirituality, intuition, caring for other humans and the planet, warmth, compassion, and human expression in its most spontaneous form can prevail. The culture of the heart is anchored in the ancestral, in the earth, in traditions and values transmitted from generation to generation. It is the type of culture prevailing in our Latin American countries, where feminine energy prevails, again not because of gender, but because of the predominance of that which cannot be measured through hard metrics nor explained through logic.

No culture is better than another; they are simply different, and each has a role. In reality, each person, each community, and each country demonstrate a certain degree of each of these cultures. There are no cultures exclusively of the mind or exclusively of the heart, but there are cultures where one predominates over the other. Even so, it's not about the geographical region or race you ancestrally descend from, but about the energy you emanate, the type of culture you vibrate in your daily work in the world. It's not a fixed concept but rather a continuously evolving experience.

At this moment, the culture of the mind predominates in the United States. And the global context that originated with the Industrial Revolution helped make that happen. The global demand for technology, scientific advances, and the pursuit of increased productivity positioned the culture of the mind as the dominant model, driving the hegemony of this country as one of the trailblazers in this type of culture. For a long time, the model seemed to work. However, those of us who come from the culture of the heart know that something is not right and feel that we don't quite fit into this cultural model. Something seems to be missing. It makes sense; we come from a different cultural model. Do you understand why, decade after decade, you may still feel you are experiencing a continuous cultural shock?

As mentioned above, we are witnessing the first steps of an unprecedented transformation. A term that is used to describe the change that has already begun is hybridization. Researched by Homi Bhabha, this word refers to creating a new culture from the encounter of two different ones. In horticulture, the term refers to the crossing of two species to form a third. Transferring this idea to the emergence of a third culture born from merging the cultures of the mind and the heart, we can expect to witness linguistic, cultural, and political influences from one culture into the other, as well as changes in ways of being and thinking that will end in the construction of a new culture where we will find more points of unity than of separation.

This does not mean that we will all think alike or become an indistinct group of identical human beings, but rather that we will appreciate and respect what makes each person unique and unrepeatable. We will accept what we bring to the table and what others bring, even if different, and see its value for our collective advancement and progress. In the same way, as we generally adopt new characteristics that we find beneficial, those of us who come from the culture of the heart will continue to incorporate aspects of the culture of the mind that can help us move more assertively in our workspaces and those who come from the culture of the mind will begin to adopt values and ways of being related with intuition, compassion, human connection and the success of the collective over the individual.

To do this, we are called to overcome our historical tendency towards domination, where the dominant culture remains inflexible and where the emerging culture is expected to set aside its ways to adopt the dominant culture. Those of us who come from the emerging culture of the heart must overcome the mistaken belief that what we bring to the table is not valuable. As a Latina executive at a global technology company told me, «We have qualities that non-Latino white Americans generally don't have, but we have been told that those qualities are not advantages, but problems or distractions.»

As an agent of change, you can become a pioneer in the mission of uniting both cultures. That's why I want to share with you the experience of those who, coming from the culture of the heart, became pioneers in navigating the culture of the mind.

THE VIEW FROM THE TOP

—Many Latino executives I've interacted with don't show our Latino values; they don't seem to represent them. They come across as rather cold, mental, and distant —Claudia, a Latina executive in the Human Resources and Diversity space, told me—. It seems they had to change their values to grow and succeed because otherwise, they wouldn't have made it.

I think most of us have noticed it. Latinos and Latinas who reach positions of power can express the characteristics of the culture of the mind. However, in private, in their homes, with their friends, or even in conversations with other Latinos, they may relax and let their true selves out, the one that comes from the culture of the heart.

But as Claudia said, «If we reach those leadership positions and can't bring what makes us unique and special, then what?» Before drawing our conclusions, let's see how the experience feels from the top, in the words of a Latina executive who has reached that space. This woman, whom we will call Virginia, explained in a moment of vulnerability exactly how she feels about modifying her way of being to keep her job and continue growing.

—I realized that the higher you go, the lonelier you are. When I was younger, I had more people, more Latinos, and more warmth around me. The higher you go, the colder everything gets, with that feeling that you must constantly watch your back. I feel that anything I do can put my career at risk —Virginia told me that morning when we met for coffee. Her expression was sad, like someone who wanted to try it differently but had to amalgamate with the environment for survival—. On the one hand, the company I work for insists and even pressures us to say that we can bring our authentic selves to work. With other Latino executives we talk about how if we had brought our authentic selves to these spaces, we really wouldn't be where we are.

Virginia told me about her daily battles, her lack of belonging, and her exhaustion from constantly having to watch what she says or does. After this conversation, I was left thinking about how much we tend to judge these individuals, labeling them as traitors to our culture while we are unaware of all they have to confront daily. Virginia helped me see the high price paid by the first ones to enter into spaces of power within the culture of the mind. At the end of the meeting with Virginia, I was left with a feeling of gratitude.

THE EXPERIENCE OF THE YOUNGER ONES

Our young Latinos will continue to enter the workforce in droves, especially our Latino Generation Z, whose ages range from 12 to 26 years old. With this generation, I believe we will finally reach the tipping point for our community when many of us realize our power and begin to exercise it confidently. The opportunity lies not only in what these young people can do for themselves but in all we can achieve together if we understand and support them.

Today, one in four Gen Z in the United States is Latino or Latina. That's equivalent to millions! Almost 90% of them were born here, perfectly handling the language and culture. Our community will face a historic opportunity with this generation: to go from being working bees and consumers whose purchases drive the American economy to leaders and directors who write the game's rules.

Dr. Patty Delgado, co-founder of El Puente Institute, has been researching our younger Latinos for years and shared some valuable information with me.

—Our Latino Gen Z does not feel forced to choose which cultural identity they belong to, nor do they carry the expectation that they need to decide between one or the other —Dr. Delgado said—. Unlike many Latinos from previous generations, such as Generation X or Baby Boomers, who were born in the United States and learned or simply accepted they had no choice but to decide between being American or being Latino, our young approach their identity more progressively —she added—. They don't choose; they take it all. They integrate the multiple facets of their cultural identity as part of who they are.

In other words, our young Latinos naturally integrate the culture of the mind and the culture of the heart. They use their American power when necessary and their Latino cultural power as they deem appropriate. By not feeling pressured to choose, they carry a toolbox from which they can extract the cultural aspect that best suits their needs at any given moment.

One of the great barriers that hinder the advancement of these young people seems to come from within our community. Dr. Patty Delgado shared an important insight:

—Sometimes, our young Latinos cannot find their voice within their families or our community due to the cultural narrative and value of *respeto* (respect). This represents our community's high appreciation for specific individuals because of their age, formal authority, or economic and social power, which creates a hierarchical way of thinking. Our cultural respect for elders or those who occupy spaces of authority causes us to cut off the initiative, perspectives, and ideas of younger people without allowing them to speak or participate in important issues and decisions.

This happens both in our homes and in the organizations we belong to. We can deprive these young people of the opportunity to express their voices, experiences, and points of view, or when they do, we can interrupt or ignore them.

Dr. Delgado told me about a personal example:

—One afternoon, we discussed racism at a family gathering, and the younger ones, who are Gen Z, wanted to speak and give their opinion. However, while they tried to raise their hands, speak, and get everyone's attention, the adults kept talking loudly without giving them space. I had to take advantage of a brief pause during the conversation to ask the other adults to stop and listen to what our young people wanted to tell us because, due to the cultural value of *respeto*, they had remained silent and were no longer trying to participate.

An apparently small experience like this can significantly impact our younger generation. As parents, educators, mentors, and members of the older generations in the Latino community, it is our responsibility to give space to the younger generations so that they can express their opinions and perspectives. We must intentionally invite them to participate and create a space for their voices. If they don't find that voice among us, their family, and the community, they may not see it anywhere else.

—We must give young people the opportunity to be the change we want for our community —Dr. Patty told me—. We have the responsibility to create those spaces for them to develop their voices and stand up to express their beliefs so that the narrative of *respeto* shifts from respect for elders or those in power to respect for diverse opinions from all ages. That is the new narrative of *respeto* that we need to consciously and deliberately develop and celebrate.

As our Gen Z continues to find its voice and place, the creation of a third culture will accelerate exponentially. In the meantime, let's continue to be pioneers in creating that third culture. If you wonder how we will do it, let me share about some trailblazing Latinas who are already doing it.

THE THIRD CULTURE IS ALREADY UNDERWAY

Viviana, an executive at a global technology company, shared an interesting story as a panelist at an event I attended. In her department, in the few minutes the team had before starting a meeting, all they would talk about was American football and baseball. Half the room participated in the conversation, and the other half was left out, unable to follow the discussion thread until one day Viviana decided to take action.

—Guys, baseball is great and a fascinating topic, but how about today we talk about something fun we did over the weekend? —she suggested to her co-workers. From that day on, the first minutes of the meeting were used for a different type of dialogue—. Now, everyone could participate, and no one was left out. We also started to get to know each other more deeply. I took that action after consulting with my mentor. I wanted to modify the «culture of a few» to make it inclusive of many, and I started with what I had in front of me.

Influencing the culture around us is possible if we start doing it from our place and with what we have in front of us at that moment. Never underestimate the power of small beginnings! Viviana is not the only one. In the following pages, I will introduce two other pioneers who have created the third culture in their workplaces. Let's first meet Diana Good Solís and then Adriana Dawson.

—My value system is mixed, a blend of both cultures —Diana Good Solís told me. The daughter of a white non-Latina mother and a Mexican father, she grew up with a foot in each culture. Nowadays, she navigates both the cultures of the mind and of the heart in her professional life. As the executive director of Acceleration Academies, Diana works on one side with several white non-Latino leaders, and on the other hand, she interacts with educators and young students, many of whom are Latino—. The cultural differences between the group of white leaders and the young Latinos who benefit from our work are significant —she continued— and part of my role is to build a bridge between both cultures so that our work is more effective.

During her school visits, Diana noticed that Latino students sat at the back and remained silent when the teacher invited them to participate. The teachers thought this was a problem of lack of interest, but Diana knew that what was taking place had to do with the cultural narrative of *respeto a la maestra* (respect to the teacher), which often means lowering one's head and not raising one's voice too much.

—It's not like that —Diana patiently explained to them—. These students don't demonstrate their interest and leadership in the same way as Anglo-Saxons do. We are facing a different culture, and you, as an educator, can create the space for them to trust and open up, participate, and dare to step out of their comfort zone.

—I learned that I am here to invite leaders and educators who have not had the experiences that our young Latinos went through and who don't fully understand our culture. Due to their lack of cultural understanding, they can reach wrong conclusions; that's why being a bridge between both cultures is about educating people on the differences that they do not perceive —Diana explained.

Diana was aware of our society's tendency towards domination, for example, by demanding that only one of the groups adapt to the other instead of meeting halfway.

—We cannot demand that young Latinos change to adjust to Anglo-Saxon ideals that define the correct way to present themselves, speak, and show leadership and commitment. We must allow them their space to express themselves, and that implies that non-Latino leaders must also change their ways to better work with these young people.

Diana possesses a very calming and poised way of speaking. I imagine her in leadership meetings sitting at the head of the table, surrounded by white non-Latino directors and leaders, and working with patience, firmness, and compassion to change how they see things.

—I lead them to take off the glasses they have been wearing for a very long time, so they dare ask themselves: «What could we be missing here?,» «What is it that we are not seeing because we grew up in different spaces?,» «What is my privilege not allowing me to see?»

Towards the end of our conversation, Diana looked me straight in the eye and said:

—The system must change and adapt, not just Latinos.

That is what creating the third culture is all about. Any similarity between classrooms and our workspaces is no coincidence!

Adriana Dawson, who we introduced before, is another pioneer in the creation of the third culture. A leader in a renowned phone company, she defines herself as a *cultural broker* because she manages both cultures in her personal and professional life.

Adriana was born in the United States to parents who immigrated from Colombia when there was not much support for immigrant families. Working in factories and surrounded by other Latinos, they were not exposed to English, so Adriana became the house's adult at six or seven years old.

—Letters would arrive in the mail, and they would ask me, «Adriana, what does this say?» They would take me out of school to accompany them to the doctor or to run important errands, so I went through experiences that made me an adult very early on, exposing me to the discrimination against those who didn't speak English or didn't know how to navigate this system.

Those experiences were key to Adriana's awareness of the disconnect between the two cultures. Today, she uses those past experiences as important assets in her role as a cultural broker.

—At work, I have courageous conversations where I suggest to others: «If you let me, I'm going to take you to my reality and share with you how I see it from my viewpoint, through my lenses.» I ask them if they are open to projecting themselves to see through the experiences of others, and at the end, I ask them: «What would you have done in that situation? How would you have felt? How would it have impacted you?»

Adriana participates in the creation of a third culture by influencing the thinking of her coworkers and leaders. She helps them understand the Latino mindset and what that means when training a sales team, launching a multicultural marketing plan, or planning how to reach our community more effectively.

ACT OF HEALTHY REBELLION

Make a list of the tools you acquired from the cultures of the mind and the heart. Respond:

Which of these tools do I want to use to advance a cause I am passionate about?

_____

_____

_____

_____

—Instead of getting emotional, I remain calm and tell them, "Let's do it together!" I also seek to understand their viewpoints and why they feel what they feel. These are conversations with empathy and courage.

WHEN WILL WE SEE A CHANGE AT SCALE?

I was almost finished writing this book when a wonderful event took place.

—One of the variables we analyze is how individualistic or collectivistic a culture is, and for the United States, we noticed that although the culture continues to be individualistic, there has been a sizable change towards collectivism —Dr. Lisa DeWaard, managing director of The Culture Factor, told me.

The way my path crossed with hers seems coincident, although I don't believe in such events. A friend had posted on LinkedIn about the different cultures that inhabit this land, and because of my comment on that post, Dr. DeWaard contacted me.

—Let me think for a moment —I requested—. Are you saying you measured a change towards collectivism in the United States, the predominant cultural trait in Latin American countries? —I asked.

—That's right! —she replied.

I don't know who was happier, her or me.

Those of us who are agents of change giving our best to transform a system that seems to resist change need proof that our efforts are worthwhile and working. At the perfect moment, the evidence appeared.

The company where Lisa works uses Geert Hofstede's Six Dimensions of National Culture, which measures attributes that make cultures different. These variables are individualism/collectivism, power distance, motivation towards achievement and success, uncertainty avoidance, indulgence/restraint, and long/short-term orientation.

Individualism/collectivism, the variable where the most significant change occurred in the United States, measures the degree of interdependence a society maintains among its members. In an individualistic society, people care for themselves and their immediate family. In a collectivist society, people also belong to groups that care for them in exchange for their loyalty. In the collectivist culture, there is more of a group-oriented mentality, with all this implies in daily life.

Historically, the United States scored 91 points on the scale from 1 to 100 that measures collectivism and individualism. The closer to 100 the score is, the more individualistic the culture. The closer to 1, the more collectivist. This means that with a 91, the United States was among the most individualistic cultures on the planet. In 2023, Lisa's company took a new measurement, and the United States' score dropped to 60, placing it almost halfway between an individualistic and a collectivist culture. For a point of comparison, Mexico scored 34, which places this country as highly collectivist.

In other words, the United States has moved from such high individualism to position itself closer to a collectivist culture like the Mexican one and other Latin American cultures. The story these numbers tell us is truly fascinating: the creation of the third culture is already underway.

—There is no right or wrong type of culture in these measurements —Lisa reminded me—. Simply, the different values help us understand what each culture brings. Additionally, understanding these differences allows us to be more patient and compassionate towards others.

Patience and compassion. We definitely need more of that!

Change will not stop here. In the coming years, we will have the opportunity to continue healing our division and sense of separation, and to form alliances of cooperation with other groups that we may see as separate and different today. For this to happen, we need to proudly acknowledge what we bring to the table and recognize that we can learn a lot from those different from us; in the same way, they can learn from what we have to offer. The puzzle will only be complete once all the pieces, the heart and the mind, fall in place.

In the meantime, let's continue growing and contributing all our greatness. Let's overcome thought and behavior patterns that no longer serve us, giving birth to the freest, most conscious, and elevated versions of ourselves. Let's keep mentoring and sponsoring other Latinos and Latinas, holding the door open as we push up and pull up. And as our ultimate act of healthy rebellion, right here and right now, let's embody the best of what the cultures of the heart and mind offer. I'm convinced that the world has yet to see all that we are capable of. Let's not deprive those around us of the opportunity to experience who we are and what we offer. The best is yet to come, and we can build it together.

LESSONS LEARNED

- As we let our authentic cultural essence come to light, heal our self-esteem, appreciate who we are, and demonstrate the values of the culture of the heart, we will positively impact our organizations and communities, transforming the very foundations of society.

- Those of us who come from the culture of the heart will incorporate more aspects of the culture of the mind to more assertively navigate our workspaces, and those who come from the culture of the mind will adopt values and ways of being around deeper human connection, intuition, compassion, and prioritizing the collective over the individual.

- We are invited to overcome our historical tendency towards domination, in which the dominant culture remains inflexible while the emerging culture is expected to fully adopt the dominant one.

- The United States has moved from a high degree of individualism to position itself halfway closer to a collectivist culture, like those in Latin America. The story these numbers tell us is fascinating: the creation of the third culture is already underway.

- In the coming years, we will have the opportunity to continue healing our divisions and forge alliances that allow us to cooperate with other groups we see as different.

- We must proudly acknowledge what we bring to the table and recognize that we can still learn a lot from those different from us, just as they can learn from what we have to offer.

Conclusion

I began this book with the promise to invite you to think differently so that you would act differently. I promised to take you by the hand so that you would see the opportunities for you and our Latino community with new eyes, so that you would dare to challenge the ancestral narratives in our collective unconscious that keep holding you back, and so that you would give yourself the freedom to proudly and authentically bring to the world the truth of who you are: an agent of change with the power to lead a historic systemic transformation.

I hope I delivered on my promise to you. This book is a travel companion, a collection of acts of healthy rebellion, and a roadmap to our individual and collective awakening. Revisit it often to reconnect with your true essence and to acknowledge how far you have come because becoming aware of your progress will fuel your confidence to keep moving forward. The world is hungry for leaders like us willing to transform themselves to revolutionize the system and drive unprecedented individual and collective change.

We know very well that we have tons of work ahead. We are only the first generations awakening to the possibility that the world around us can be different, more inclusive, warmer, and more receptive to our dreams. In the face of the many obstacles we will continue to face, remember to place yourself first and take care of yourself. Because we are on the front line of this massive transformation, the emotional, physical, mental, and spiritual demands will continue to be high. That is why creating spaces to rest, replenish, reconnect with yourself, and gather strength is critical. Don't minimize the importance of taking your time and space; do it without guilt.

On those days when the work to be done seems to exceed your strength, hold the vision of what will be possible for us all when we unite in our diversity, and keep walking towards that vision with compassion, not only for you but also for those who hurt you. Remember that we all do the best we can with what we know. If they knew better, we would have already done it.

Recently, a Latina leader who has accessed spaces of power expressed in a podcast that every time she is invited to a reception at the luxurious home of one of her husband's white non-Latino business connections, she is asked what country she is from when they notice her accent. As soon as she says «Mexican,» they take her to the kitchen to greet their Mexican kitchen staff or introduce her to their landscaping employees.

Even those with the best intentions to connect with us cannot sometimes avoid showing their biases and stereotypes, which are mostly unconscious. Let's not take it as an insult but as a powerful reminder of how far we have come and how far we can still go. We come from ancestral sacrifice and physical labor and keep progressing toward spaces of power where vital decisions are made. We beautifully converge a past of difficult trials and a future of infinite possibilities, and only by fully honoring these dissimilar parts that constitute who we are can we express our most authentic Latinidad with confidence and pride.

To conclude this book, I want to share what my friend David Clegg, a great ally in my journey, sent me some time ago. It is a fascinating millenary prophecy that invites us to dream that union in our diversity is possible and that the fusion of the best of our cultures will be a portal to live in the truth and freedom we deserve.

THE PROPHECY OF THE EAGLE AND THE CONDOR

This prophecy, which seems to originate from the Amazon jungle and dates back two thousand years, tells that since time immemorial, our societies have taken separate paths, forming two different communities: the people of the eagle and the people of the condor.

The people of the eagle, oriented towards the intellectual, masculine, and industrial, represent the culture of the mind. The people of the condor, oriented towards ancestral, intuitive, and feminine, represent the culture of the heart. Interestingly, the eagle is the most depicted bird in North America and is featured on the Great Seal of the United States. The condor, on the other hand, is the largest flying bird in South America.

The prophecy indicates that the paths of the eagle and the condor would not cross for many years until the Fifth Pachakuti, when they finally met, with almost devastating consequences. The eagle would be so strong that it would practically lead the condor to extinction. For centuries, the culture of the mind became dominant, pushing the culture of the heart to its near demise.

It also indicates that this Fifth Pachakuti would create a portal so that one day, the eagle and the condor can fly together in the sky, uniting to create a superior human consciousness. This would be the encounter between heart and mind, art and science, the spiritual with the material, and the feminine with the masculine, to radically transform our society.

This oracle concludes with the prediction that when the eagle and the condor finally unite, the spirit of peace will set on this land, and a new era will have begun for all.

Let's release the ancestral impulse for domination and for pointing out what separates us. Let's remember that the cultures of the mind and the heart are not restricted by geographical regions or the races from which we descend but manifest in the energy we radiate and vibrate at each moment. Let's bring out the best of what the cultures of the heart and mind offer and walk in a direction that brings us closer together. As this happens, the transformation in our families, communities, organizations, and countries will be so profound that, here and now, we cannot even imagine its magnitude.

Thank you for believing that change is possible. Thank you for leading the awakening and transformation our collective has longed for centuries. Thank you for daring to be an Unbeatable Latina!

Acknowledgments

In recent years, I have been blessed to witness the healing power that sharing our most personal stories has on us, immigrant Latinas and daughters of immigrants.

Telling our stories allows us to look into our past and give a name to our experiences, which helps to heal the wounds of a journey that was plagued with trauma and difficulties. It allows us to look into our present, which helps us acknowledge our current obstacles and find unity in our common battles. It will enable us to dream of a better future, inviting us to keep sharing the roadmap of what works professionally for women like us because doing so will only accelerate our arrival into spaces of power and wealth creation.

When the opportunity of writing this book came up, I did not hesitate for a second. I knew it would be a titanic task, but the prospect of leaving a legacy for our community motivated me to embark with no hesitation on this adventure of long nights and busy weekends. My intuition told me that the individuals and stories I would encounter during the writing process would forever transform my life. My intuition was correct. A book is as transformative for the reader as it is for the writer, and there was a before and after in my life writing *Unbeatable Latinas*.

My deepest gratitude goes to my family, the pillar of my life. To my children, Valentina and Tommy, who inspire me to keep going; to my husband, Gonzalo Martín, who encourages me to pursue my dreams; to my mom, Berta Margarita Schimpf de Aloé, and to my dad, Juan Carlos Aloé, who always believe in me no matter what I decide to undertake, and to my brothers Ricardo and Julio, who continue to be a key part of my past and present, as well as my aunts, cousins, my parents-in-law Moña and Juan Carlos, my nephews and nieces, brothers and sisters-in-law, especially Caro Merlo, whose incredible support from Argentina was a driving force for me to keep dreaming with this project. To my dear friends Melba Alhonte and Joan Witkowskie, whose guidance and support are bright lights in my life.

At critical moments in my journey, I was blessed to cross paths with allies and sponsors who opened life-changing doors of opportunity for me. For this book, that visionary who committed to bringing our stories to life and sharing a roadmap for our success was Cristóbal Pera, vice president of Editorial Planeta in the United States, who believed in my work from day one and made it possible for this transformative project to materialize. Without the support of Cristóbal Pera and the entire amazing Planeta team, including Fernanda Martínez, who contributed invaluably to the editing, and Astrid Harders Gómez, Helen Hernández Hormilla and Mónica Vega Velásquez, in charge of marketing, this work would not be in your hands today.

My special thanks to all the women and men, Latinos and non-Latinos, who during the writing process shared with me their life experiences, their barriers, their achievements, and their process of personal transformation to become the influential change agents that they are: Adriana Dawson, Adrienne Valencia García, Alice Rodríguez, Ana Valdez, Andrew Rodríguez, Carla Dodds, Carolina Alarco, Claudia Romo Edelman, Claudia Vázquez, Cynthia Kleinbaum, Cynthia Trejo, David Morales, Diana Good Solís, Diana Peña, Dulce Orozco, Elisa Charters, Elizabeth Nieto, Esther Aguilera, Francis Hondal, Gabriel Perez, Dr. Gail Ayala Taylor, Hady Mendez, Dr. Ivonne Díaz-Claisse, J. C.

González-Mendez, Jessica Rodríguez, Joan Witkowskie, Joanie Gines, Juliette Gebken-Mayi, Kat Vera, Laura Rivera, Dr. Lisa DeWaard, Lisa, Lory Burgos, Lucy, Lupita Colmenero, Lyanne Alfaro, Manuel Velásquez, Marcela Gómez, Marie Quintana, Dr. Marisol Capellán, Melanie Sole, Melba Alhonte, Millie Guzmán, Mónica Martínez Milán, Mónica Márquez, Nadya Ramos, Natalia Ariza, Natasha Tous, Ofelia Kumpf, Dr. Patty Delgado, Phyllis Barajas, Raquel K., Robert Bard, Roxanne Martinez, Santi Strasser, Sara, Silvana Montenegro, Sol Trujillo, Traci Ruiz, Teri Arvesú González y Yai Vargas.

Thank you, dear reader. The world needs courageous leaders like you, committed to profoundly transforming themselves to ignite the most extraordinary systemic transformation we have ever imagined.

And finally, thank you, God, for being my partner. I trust the best is yet to come for us all.

Bibliography

INTRODUCTION

- Tendency of the Latino community to work hard:
  C., F. (2023, May 3). *Los laboriosos latinoamericanos: mucho trabajo, pocos beneficios*. Diario Libre. https://www.diariolibre.com/actualidad/reportajes/2023/05/03/laboriosos-latinoamericanos-mucho-trabajo-pocos-beneficios/2304504
- Roots of the mental health crisis in the Latino community:
  Franco, M. E. (2021, May 13). *Latino mental health crisis grows*. Axios.com. https://www.axios.com/2021/05/13/latino-mental-health-crisis-covid-pandemic?utm_source=newsletter&utm_medium=email&utm_campaign=newsletter_axioslatino&stream=science
- Statistics that reflect both our power and our absence in leadership, decision-making, and wealth-creation spaces:
  Datasets about the U.S. Hispanic community. (2024). https://drive.google.com/file/d/1-Z8pIErY3Q786mt4XQcZB-ZunhEI_9L1/view

CHAPTER 1

- Population of Latino women in 2022 by Latin American country:
  Población, mujeres - Latin America & Caribbean. (2024). World Bank Open Data. https://datos.bancomundial.org/indicator/SP.POP.TOTL.FE.IN?locations=ZJ
- Latino population in the United States according to the 2010 Census:
  2010 Census Briefs. (2011, May). *The Hispanic population: 2010*. Census.gov. https://www.census.gov/history/pdf/c2010br-04-092020.pdf

- Projection of the Latino population in the United States between 2017 and 2060:
US Census Bureau. (2018). *Hispanic population to reach 111 million by 2060.* https://www.census.gov/library/visualizations/2018/comm/hispanic-projected-pop.html
- Projection of workforce growth in the United States by race/ethnicity:
Hernández, K., Garcia, D., Nazario, P., Rios, M., & Domínguez-Villegas, R. (2021, June 14). *How the pandemic revealed historic disadvantages and heightened economic hardship.* Ucla.edu. https://latino.ucla.edu/wp-content/uploads/2021/10/Latinas-Exiting-the-Workforce.pdf
- Statistics of Latino entrepreneurship compared to other ethnic and racial groups:
The 2019 State of Women-Owned Businesses Report. (2019). Ventureneer.com. https://ventureneer.com/wp-content/uploads/2019/10/Final-2019-state-of-women-owned-businesses-report.pdf
- Latino representation in managerial and executive positions:
Guyn, J., & Fraser, J. (2022, August 2). *Only two Latinas have been CEO of a Fortune 500 company. Why do so few Hispanic women make it to the top?* USA Today. https://www.usatoday.com/story/money/2022/08/02/hispanic-latina-business-demographics-executive/10157271002/?gnt-cfr=1
- Latina pay gap:
Latinas aren't paid fairly—and that's just the tip of the iceberg. Lean In. https://leanin.org/data-about-the-gender-pay-gap-for-latinas
- Accumulated wealth per household by race/ethnicity:
Kent, A. H., & Ricketts, L. R. (2024, February 7). *U.S. Wealth Inequality: Gaps Remain Despite Widespread Wealth Gains.* Stlouisfed.org. https://www.stlouisfed.org/open-vault/2024/feb/us-wealth-inequality-widespread-gains-gaps-remain#%3A%7E%3Atext%3DHispanic%20Families%27%20Wealth%2Cdollar%20of%20white%20median%20wealth
- About the collective unconscious (Carl Jung):
Inconsciente colectivo. Wikipedia, The Free Encyclopedia. https://es.wikipedia.org/w/index.php?title=Inconsciente_colectivo&oldid=159445108

CHAPTER 2

- Educational levels of the Latino community:
Román, E. (2023, July 14). *Latinos aren't represented in higher education. Here's how to fix that.* The Boston Globe. https://www.bostonglobe.com/2023/07/14/opinion/latinos-arent-represented-higher-education-heres-how-fix-that/

- Women apply for jobs only if we meet 100% of the requirements (men apply with 60%):
  Lean in for Graduates. Lean In. https://leanin.org/graduates

CHAPTER 3

- Trends and perceptions within the Latino community, including our level of unity behind one voice:
  Untapped potential: The Hispanic talent advantage. IBM. https://www.ibm.com/thought-leadership/institute-business-value/en-us/report/hispanic-talent-advantage
- Existence of subcultures within the Latino community:
  Schaeffer, K. (2023, September 5). *Who is Hispanic?* Pew Research Center. https://www.pewresearch.org/short-reads/2023/09/05/who-is-hispanic/
- Presence and incidence of Latinos according to their country of origin in the different cities of the United States:
  Kent, D. (2023, August 16). *11 facts about Hispanic origin groups in the U.S.* Pew Research Center. https://www.pewresearch.org/short-reads/2023/08/16/11-facts-about-hispanic-origin-groups-in-the-us/
- About our sense of belonging to the United States based on how many generations we have been in the country:
  Kent, D. (2020, September 24). *The ways Hispanics describe their identity vary across immigrant generations.* Pew Research Center. https://www.pewresearch.org/short-reads/2020/09/24/the-ways-hispanics-describe-their-identity-vary-across-immigrant-generations/
- Use of the Spanish and English language in the Latino community:
  [Krogstad, J. M. (2015, March 24). *A majority of English-speaking Hispanics in the U.S. are bilingual.* Pew Research Center. https://www.pewresearch.org/short-reads/2015/03/24/a-majority-of-english-speaking-hispanics-in-the-u-s-are-bilingual/
- Educational attainment by race or ethnicity:
  Educational attainment statistics [2023]: *Levels by demographic.* (2020, June 25). Education Data Initiative. https://educationdata.org/education-attainment-statistics

CHAPTER 4

- Statistics on the Afro-Latino community in the United States:
  Blazina, C. (2022, May 2). *About 6 million U.S. adults identify as Afro-Latino.*

Pew Research Center. https://www.pewresearch.org/short-reads/2022/05/02/about-6-million-u-s-adults-identify-as-afro-latino/
- Experiences of discrimination and bias by race and ethnicity:
Noe-Bustamante, L., Gonzalez-Barrera, A., Edwards, K., Mora, L., & Lopez, M. H. (2021, November 4). 4. *Measuring the racial identity of Latinos.* Pew Research Center. https://www.pewresearch.org/race-and-ethnicity/2021/11/04/measuring-the-racial-identity-of-latinos/
- Educational level of Afro-Latina women compared to the general female Latina cohort:
Galdamez, M. (2023, April 20). *Centering black latinidad.* Latino Policy & Politics Institute. https://latino.ucla.edu/research/centering-black-latinidad/

CHAPTER 5

- Statistics on first generation in college:
Redford, J., Raplh, J., & Hoyer, K. M. (2017, September). *First-generation and continuing-generation college students: A comparison of high school and postsecondary experiences.* Nces.ed.gov. https://nces.ed.gov/pubs2018/2018009.pdf
- Statistics of female Latino community entrepreneurship:
The 2023 impact of women-owned businesses. (2023, September 15). Ventureneer.com. https://ventureneer.com/wp-content/uploads/2023/10/IWOB-Hispanic-Latino-Women-Owned-Businesses-230912_Final.pdf
- Corporate purchasing from minority-owned businesses:
2022 state of supplier diversity report. (2022, March 15). Supplier.Io. https://supplier.io/resources/reports/2022-state-of-supplier-diversity-report
- Changes in the perception of female talent capabilities:
Novotny, A. (2023, March 23). *Women leaders make work better. Here's the science behind how to promote them.* Apa.org. https://www.apa.org/topics/women-girls/female-leaders-make-work-better?utm_source=linkedin&utm_medium=social&utm_campaign=apa-leadership&utm_content=female-leaders-make-work-better

CHAPTER 6

- Brain functioning and formation of beliefs that impact our reality:
Vilhauer, J. (2020, September 27). *How your thinking creates your reality.* Psychology Today. https://www.psychologytoday.com/us/blog/living-forward/202009/how-your-thinking-creates-your-reality

- The power of meditation, inner silence, and slowing down to know who we are, and to love ourselves and others:
  D'Ors, P. (2022). *La meditación es un camino radical para el autoconocimiento.* Aprendemos Juntos. https://www.youtube.com/watch?v=pG-7mMRYTP6Q

CHAPTER 7

- The ethnic and racial diversity of executives drives higher profits in companies:
  Dixon-Fyle, S., Dolan, K., Hunt, D. V., & Prince, S. (2020). *Diversity wins: How inclusion matters.* McKinsey & Company. https://www.mckinsey.com/featured-insights/diversity-and-inclusion/diversity-wins-how-inclusion-matters
- Latino talent barriers to bringing their whole selves to the workplace:
  Hewlett, S. A., Allwood, N., & Sherbin, L. (2016, October 11). *U.S. Latinos feel they can't be themselves at work.* Harvard Business Review. https://hbr.org/2016/10/u-s-latinos-feel-they-cant-be-themselves-at-wor
- Emotional and physical health costs for those who feel they must repress and suppress their personality:
  Elsig, C. M. (2022, January 24). *The dangers of suppressing emotions.* The CALDA Clinic. https://caldaclinic.com/dangers-of-suppressing-emotions/
- America Ferrera and the power of our true selves to transform the system:
  Ferrera, A. (2019, May 23). *My identity is a superpower -- not an obstacle.* https://www.ted.com/talks/america_ferrera_my_identity_is_a_superpower_not_an_obstacle/transcript?language=en
- How coming out of the closet (or not) can impact our professional life:
  Hewlett, S. A. (2011, July 18). *The cost of closeted employees.* Harvard Business Review. https://hbr.org/2011/07/the-cost-of-closeted-employees

CHAPTER 8

- Why it is harmful to call «syndrome» the impostor syndrome:
  Jamison, L. (2023, February 6). *Why everyone feels like they're faking it.* New Yorker. https://www.newyorker.com/magazine/2023/02/13/the-dubious-rise-of-impostor-syndrome
- Commencement speech delivered by Reshma Saujani:
  Saujani, R. (2024). *Imposter Syndrome Is A Scheme.* Smith College. https://www.youtube.com/watch?v=BoHDDgeQtlc

CHAPTER 9

- Psychic legacies and trauma are passed down from adults to children:
  Castelloe, M. S. (2020, September 23). *Cómo se transmite el trauma entre generaciones.* Psychology Today. https://www.psychologytoday.com/es/blog/como-se-transmite-el-trauma-entre-generaciones
- Women only apply for jobs if they meet 100% of the requirements:
  Mohr, T. S. (2014, August 25). *Why women don't apply for jobs unless they're 100% qualified?* Harvard Business Review. https://hbr.org/2014/08/why-women-dont-apply-for-jobs-unless-theyre-100-qualified
- Women receive unclear or insufficiently detailed feedback:
  Language bias in performance feedback. Textio. https://textio.com/feedback-bias
- Biases in feedback towards Latinos or African Americans:
  Makoni, A. (2022, July 20). *Black and latinx employees face bias in job performance feedback, study finds.* POCIT. https://peopleofcolorintech.com/front/black-and-latinx-employees-face-bias-in-job-performance-feedback-study-finds/

CHAPTER 10

- Barriers that women face at work, including the «broken rung»:
  Women in the Workplace 2023: Key findings & takeaways. Lean In. https://leanin.org/women-in-the-workplace?gclid=CjwKCAiAjfyqBhAsEiwA-UdzJDri9sOYo3n8MTmAbXTxHu8AHa5mkbb8yUDnYsjVB6tGtnz_8HWrgxoC-mY4QAvD_BwE
- Census statistics regarding businesses with and without employees:
  Total Nonemployer Establishments. (2024). Census.gov. https://www.census.gov/quickfacts/fact/note/US/NES010220
- Differences in motivations and interests by generation:
  Generational Differences in the Workplace. Purdueglobal.edu. https://www.purdueglobal.edu/education-partnerships/generational-workforce-differences-infographic/
- Interests and preferences of millennials in the workplace:
  Gallup, Inc. (2018, August 1). *How millennials want to work and live.* Gallup.com; Gallup. https://www.gallup.com/workplace/238073/millennials-work-live.aspx
- Leadership and management style of millennials:
  Millennials are managers now. (2020, March 10). Zapier.com; Zapier. https://zapier.com/blog/millennial-managers-report/

- Characteristics that make women more effective leaders than men:
Kruse, K. (2023, March 31). *New research: Women more effective than men in all leadership measures*. Forbes. https://www.forbes.com/sites/kevinkruse/2023/03/31/new-research-women-more-effective-than-men-in-all-leadership-measures/?sh=3ee064fa577a

CHAPTER 11

- Tasks and commitments that tend to disproportionately fall on women:
Women in the Workplace 2023. Leanin.org and McKinsey & Company. https://womenintheworkplace.com/
- How women in leadership positions work more on diversity efforts and other unpaid tasks:
Yee, L. (2021, October 19). *The «third shift» matters - and women do more of it*. Fastcompany.com. https://www.fastcompany.com/90687404/the-third-shift-matters-and-women-do-more-of-it
- Statistics on exhaustion experienced by women, men, and young people:
Smith, M. (2023, March 14). *Burnout is on the rise worldwide—and Gen Z, young millennials and women are the most stressed*. CNBC. https://www.cnbc.com/2023/03/14/burnout-is-on-the-rise-gen-z-millennials-and-women-are-the-most-stressed.html
- About the «maternal penalty» and the additional barriers we face when we decide to become mothers:
Personal finance. (2011, September 8). Business Insider. https://www.businessinsider.com/personal-finance

CHAPTER 12

- The «P. I. E.» framework by Harvey Coleman, on key pillars of our professional success:
Hatler, R. (2021, February 24). *The P.I.E theory of success - performance, Image, Exposure*. Arrowhead Consulting | Business Consulting Tulsa; Arrowhead Consulting. https://arrowheadconsulting.com/2021/02/24/the-p-i-e-theory-of-success-performance-image-exposure/
- Putnam's social capital and how we can build it for our professional growth:
Kiechel, W. (2000, July 1). *The new new capital thing*. Harvard Business Review. https://hbr.org/2000/07/the-new-new-capital-thing

- About the lack of mentorship for women in workspaces:
  Neal, S., Boatman, J., & Miller, L. (2013, April 9). *Mentoring women in the workplace: A global study.* Ddiworld.com. https://www.ddiworld.com/research/mentoring-women-in-the-workplace
- Reluctance of male executives to meet alone or travel with women from their workplaces:
  The number of men who are uncomfortable mentoring women is growing. Lean In. https://leanin.org/article/the-number-of-men-who-are-uncomfortable-mentoring-women-is-growing

CHAPTER 13

- Carla Harris' method for requesting sponsorship from her leaders:
  Connley, C. (2023, February 23). *Why This Wall Street Executive Says «Hard Work Will Not Complete Your Success Equation.»* Chief.com. https://chief.com/articles/wall-street-executive-hard-work-will-not-complete-success-equation?utm_campaign=2023-02-23-editorial&utm_medium=social&utm_source=linkedin&utm_content=cta&1

CHAPTER 14

- Most frequent age in the Latino community in the United States:
  2023 LDC Fast Facts. Latinodonorcollaborative.org. https://latinodonorcollaborative.org/reports/2023-ldc-fast-facts/
- About HISPA's (Hispanics Inspiring Students' Performance and Achievement) mission:
  Annual review. (2017, February 6). HISPA. https://www.hispa.org/annual_review/
- DEI's (Diversity, Equity and Inclusion) evolution in the last years:
  Chen, T.-P., & Weber, L. (2023, July 21). *The Rise and Fall of the Chief Diversity Officer.* Wsj.com. https://www.wsj.com/business/c-suite/chief-diversity-officer-cdo-business-corporations-e110a82f?mod=hp_lead_pos9
- About LCDA (Latino Corporate Directors Association):
  Latino Corporate Directors Association. Latinocorporatedirectors.org. https://latinocorporatedirectors.org/
- Latino representation in Fortune 1000 boards of directors:
  Latino representation on Fortune 1000 boards. Latinocorporatedirectors.org. https://latinocorporatedirectors.org/latinorepresentationonfortune1000boards.php

CHAPTER 15

- Women and minorities are viewed with suspicion when we participate in promoting diversity in our spaces:
Johnson, S. K., & Hekman, D. R. (2016, March 23). *Women and minorities are penalized for promoting diversity.* Harvard business review. https://hbr.org/2016/03/women-and-minorities-are-penalized-for-promoting-diversity

CHAPTER 16

- Statistics on the progress of African American talent in leadership spaces:
Smith, R. A., & Fuhrmans, V. (2023, November 28). *What a Drop in Promotions for Black Workers Says About Corporate Diversity Efforts.* Wsj.com. https://www.wsj.com/business/fewer-black-professionals-are-getting-promoted-into-management-reversing-trend-e2e002d5
- Statistics on racial and ethnic diversity within the Jewish community:
How Many Jews of Color are There? (2020, May 17). Ejewishphilanthropy.com. https://ejewishphilanthropy.com/how-many-jews-of-color-are-there/

CHAPTER 17

- Homi Bhabha's *hybridization*, or the creation of a new culture as a result of the encounter of two different cultures:
Kay, C. (2005, December). *Celso Furtado: Pioneer of Structuralist Development Theory.* Researchgate.net. https://www.researchgate.net/publication/317102764_Celso_Furtado_Pioneer_of_Structuralist_Development_Theory
- Geert Hofstede's Six Dimensions of National Culture, country comparison:
Country comparison tool. Hofstede-insights.com. https://www.hofstede-insights.com/country-comparison-tool?countries=mexico%2Cunited%2Bstates

About the author

Valeria Aloe is a consultant expert in culture and diversity, as well as a speaker, an award-winning author, and the founder of Rising Together.

The first in her family to graduate from college and access corporate spaces both in her native Argentina and in the United States, Valeria accumulates more than 20 years of experience in brand management, business development and finance in leading corporations across seven countries, including Procter & Gamble, Citibank, Reckitt Benckiser, TIAA, and PricewaterhouseCoopers.

In 2018 she launched Rising Together, a consulting and workforce development company with a mission to help close gender and leadership gaps in the Latino community. Through this company, Valeria assists Fortune 500 companies in addressing the unique cultural needs of their Latino professionals and supports their non-Latino managers and leaders in becoming more assertive mentors and sponsors of Latino talent.

Her work has been recognized with several awards, including «Top 100 Latina in the U.S. in 2023,» «Top 50 Women in Business in New Jersey in 2020,» and «5th Most Influential Hispanic in New Jersey in 2021.» Her first book, *Uncolonized Latinas*, won first place in the non-fiction category at the New York Book Festival, among 16 other national and international recognitions.

Valeria is the Vice President of Lean In Latina Surge National and serves in the Latin American and Caribbean Alumni Council of the Tuck School of Business at Dartmouth. She holds Business Administration and Finance degrees from Universidad Católica Argentina, an MBA from the Tuck School of Business at Dartmouth, and a Master's in Spiritual Sciences. She is currently pursuing a Doctorate in Spiritual Sciences.

To learn more about Valeria's work visit
www.ValeriaAloe.com